# MEETINGS WITH JESUS

# MEETINGS WITH JESUS

*Men and women from the Gospels
come face to face with the
Son of God*

*Edited by*
Patrick Whitworth

TERRA NOVA PUBLICATIONS

Published in Great Britain by
Terra Nova Publications Ltd
PO Box 2400, Bradford on Avon, Wiltshire BA15 2YN

ISBN 1-901949-11-7

Cover design: Gazelle Creative Productions
Cover printed by The Shires Press, Trowbridge, Wiltshire

Printed in Great Britain at
The Cromwell Press, Trowbridge, Wiltshire

# Contents

The Contributors      7
Foreword      9
Preface      11

## Beginnings

1   Expectation: Simeon and Anna      13
    *Jon Soper*
2   Identification: John the Baptist      19
    *Patrick Whitworth*
3   Temptation: the devil      25
    *Patrick Whitworth*
4   Vocation: Simon Peter      35
    *Patrick Whitworth*

## New Beginnings

5   Salvation: the woman at the well      43
    *Jon Soper*
6   Compassion: the widow of Nain      49
    *Nigel Rawlinson*
7   Disputation: the man born blind      55
    *Patrick Whitworth*
8   Inclusion: the Syro-Phoenician woman      63
    *Patrick Whitworth*
9   Liberation: the Gadarene demoniac      69
    *Patrick Whitworth*

10  Invitation: the rich young ruler                77
    *Patrick Whitworth*
11  Deception: the woman caught in adultery         85
    *Patrick Whitworth*
12  Adoration: Mary                                 93
    *Jon Soper*
13  Confession: at Simon's house                    99
    *Andrew Perry*

## The Beginning of the End

14  Damnation: Judas                               107
    *Patrick Whitworth*
15  Adjudication: Pilate                           115
    *Nigel Rawlinson*
16  Division: the penitent thief                   123
    *Patrick Whitworth*
17  Stupefaction: Mary Magdalene                   129
    *Sarah Couchman*
18  Hesitation: Thomas                             137
    *Patrick Whitworth*
19  Restoration: Simon Peter                       145
    *Patrick Whitworth*

## Epilogue

20  Revelation: on the road to Emmaus              153
    *Patrick Whitworth*

# Contributors

Patrick Whitworth was Curate of Holy Trinity Brompton, following a first curacy at St. Michael-le-Belfry, York, where he served under David Watson. Following eleven years as Vicar of Christ Church, Gipsy Hill, in south east London, he took up his present post as Rector of All Saints, Weston, Bath. He is a Canon of Bauchi Diocese, Northern Nigeria and is Chairman of the UK *SOMA* Council. Patrick is married to Olivia and they have four children.

Sarah Couchman is the Lay Reader at All Saints, Weston, Bath. She is married to James, who is Treasurer for the Development Project. They have a daughter.

Andrew Perry, now Vicar of Longfleet, was a Curate at All Saints, Weston, Bath (1991–1995). He is married to Fiona and they have three children.

Nigel Rawlinson is an ONSM at All Saints, Weston, Bath. He is a Consultant in the Accident and Emergency Department at Bristol Royal Infirmary, and at Weston General Hospital, Weston-Super-Mare. He is married to Pat and they have two daughters.

Jon Soper, Associate Vicar of St. Paul's, Onslow Square with St. Mary's, Bryanston Square in London, was a Curate at All Saints, Weston, Bath (1996–May 2000). He is married to Jo and they have a son.

# Foreword

The heart of the Christian faith is a relationship with God. We encounter God through encountering Jesus. *Meetings with Jesus* is the story of lives that were touched by the presence of Jesus. Tracing through the life of Christ from his presentation in the Temple to his resurrection appearances, this book illustrates the transforming power and grace of Jesus in the lives of individuals in very different settings. Patrick paints a vivid picture of these people, allowing us to identify with their need for Christ and to reflect in a deeper way upon the profound love he showed to all he met.

Patrick is a man of great vision. It is this vision that seeks to transform the local old school house into a centre for Christian activity at the heart of his community. All the royalties from this book are going to support this project.

*Nicky Gumbel*

# *Preface*

Like most local churches, we have sought to start this new millennium in an emphatic way. At the beginning of the year we joined with twenty five other local churches to present God's way to live—the Ten Commandments—to our city, with J. John's inimitable help. Later on we celebrated this new millennium in our local community with a performance of a musical account of the Bible's message called *The Promise*, composed by a member of our congregation, Margaret White. This autumn, along with many others, we 'invited the nation to supper' to take part in Alpha courses in our city. Five hundred people came to supper in our gracious Guildhall in Bath, to hear the talk, *Christianity: Boring, Untrue and Irrelevant?*

All the royalties from this little book go to help finance an extensive refurbishment of an old listed Cotswold school house into a modern church community centre. In these and other ways we are praying and working for the TRANSFORMATION of our community.

But the beginning of transformation is to be found initially in the lives of individual men, women and children as they meet Jesus. Much of Jesus' ministry took place in the context of meetings with individuals—in all kinds of settings. For most of this year we have followed a sermon series centred on many of these meetings. Each meeting with Jesus has a dominant theme, a theme that is as vital today as then. Most, but not all, of this series is reproduced here. All of the contributions are by past and present members of this church. I would like to thank them all, including Peter Norman and Peter Jones, for sharing in this project. I would also like to thank John Gilmour and Binky Clark for their help in transcription.

I am very grateful to Peter and Jane Byron-Davies for their confidence in the project, and Nicky Gumbel for his kind Foreword. Finally, I would like to thank my long-suffering wife, Olivia, and my children for putting up with numerous forays to the laptop over recent months when I might have been more sociable!

The book is dedicated to all the saints at All Saints who, like me, have been changed by a transforming meeting with Jesus Christ. Our prayer is that the transformation may continue in all of our communities and in us.

*Patrick Whitworth*
Advent Sunday 2000

# 1

# Expectation:
# Simeon and Anna

## Jon Soper

Unlike all other religions and philosophies, Christian faith is in the creator God who reveals his own nature and his purposes for us; who *speaks* to the men and women he has created. Above all, he communicates through his son Jesus Christ, who is truly God and truly man. Such faith is much more than intellectual assent; it is the mark of a *relationship* of the deepest kind, and having a 'relationship' implies having met!

The Gospels show us how people who met Jesus were profoundly affected by him. Many of the encounters described in this book were **transforming**, and they all included powerful **communication** from God.

In a most exciting way, God continues to speak through these encounters, as the Holy Spirit opens our hearts. We hear for ourselves that divine communication, and begin to know that transformation. We too can discover that to have seen Jesus is to have seen the Father.

We start by thinking of two people who met with the *baby* Jesus.

On the eighth day, when it was time to circumcise him, he was named Jesus, the name the angel had given him before he had been conceived. When the time of their purification according to the Law of Moses had been completed, Joseph and Mary took him to Jerusalem to present him to the Lord (as it is written in the Law of the Lord, "Every firstborn male is to be consecrated to the Lord"), and to offer a sacrifice in keeping with what is said in the Law of the Lord: "a pair of doves or two young pigeons."

Now there was a man in Jerusalem called Simeon, who was righteous and devout. He was waiting for the consolation of Israel, and the Holy Spirit was upon him. It had been revealed to him by the Holy Spirit that he would not die before he had seen the Lord's Christ. Moved by the Spirit, he went into the temple courts. When the parents brought in the child Jesus, to do for him what the custom of the Law required, Simeon took him in his arms and praised God, saying:

> "Sovereign Lord, as you have promised,
> you now dismiss your servant in peace.
> For my eyes have seen your salvation,
> which you have prepared in the sight of all people,
> a light for revelation to the Gentiles
> and for glory to your people Israel."

The child's father and mother marvelled at what was said about him. Then Simeon blessed them and said to Mary, his mother: "This child is destined to cause the falling and rising of many in Israel, and to be a sign that will be spoken against, so that the thoughts of many hearts will be revealed. And a sword will pierce your own soul too."

There was also a prophetess, Anna, the daughter of Phanuel, of the tribe of Asher. She was very old; she had lived with her husband seven years after her marriage, and then was a widow until she was eighty-four. She never left the temple but worshipped night and day, fasting and praying. Coming up to them at that very moment, she gave thanks to God and spoke about the child to all who were looking forward to the redemption of Jerusalem.

*Luke 2:21–38*

Jesus had a profound effect upon Simeon and Anna, even though he was a young baby; because they had now, at last, found the One they had been looking for. They had been waiting a long time for this moment. Most of us are not good at waiting, especially when we expect things to move fast. If we are waiting for a hamburger at the drive-in, we may find ourselves drumming our fingers; this is supposed to be fast food, so why is it not faster? We get more powerful computers because we want to work and play ever faster. But Simeon and Anna *waited patiently* for a long time —hoping to meet the person they really wanted to see.

Let us look at what happens in this passage. It takes us on from the Nativity, with the angels, and the shepherds going to see Jesus.

# EXPECTATION

In those times the Jewish people had three rituals following the birth of a child: after eight days the child had to be circumcised; then, within the first month if it were the first-born, five shekels were paid to the Temple for the child's redemption; finally, within the first forty days, the mother (and, in this case, both Mary and Joseph) would come for the 'purification'. So there are rituals to be performed according to the Law. When we have a first-born child these days, we have different, secular, rituals—such as phoning the relatives from hospital (and by the time you get round to the new aunts and uncles you realise that they have already heard!)

Mary and Joseph bring their first-born child to the Temple and they meet two extraordinary people. The first, Simeon, is described as 'righteous and devout' and, very unusually, the Gospel tells us that the Holy Spirit was upon him. The Spirit revealed certain things to him; he was moved by the Spirit; and he was in the Spirit when he came into the Temple. Presumably the Spirit revealed to him that this baby was the Messiah they were looking for. In the biblical record we are shown little of the Holy Spirit's activity in general revelation during the centuries immediately preceding this moment. But then Jesus is born, and an incredible explosion of Holy Spirit activity occurs. Under the leading of the Spirit, Simeon had been waiting for the consolation of Israel.

Then Mary and Joseph meet Anna, an elderly woman who was incredibly focused and dedicated. She was the kind of person who we would say today 'never misses a service', devoting herself to worship, fasting, praying, and seeking God. Now she was able and willing to speak of Jesus to 'those who looked for redemption in Jerusalem'. Both Simeon and Anna were devout, prophetic people, who were *waiting for God to speak to them.*

The words Simeon utters show that he is 'soaked' in the second half of Isaiah (chapters 40–66, especially chapter 52, which looks forward to the coming of the Messiah). The prophecies of Isaiah permeated his thinking as he meditated on the word of God—as he prayed, and as he looked forward with hope, expecting the fulfilment of prophecy. He was ready and alert for whatever God might do: sending the Messiah, bringing salvation to Israel and to the ends of the earth—as he says, in the Nunc Dimittis, '...to be a light to lighten the Gentiles' —a light for people outside the Jewish nation. This meditation on the Old Testament produced in Simeon and Anna the character of those who were ready for the Gospel—

for seeing what God was about to do; and they cherished a holy expectancy. They had been ready for a very long while.

We observe that Simeon and Anna *speak under the power of the Spirit*. When Simeon takes Jesus in his arms and looks at the baby, he knows in anticipation that this is the one for whom he has been waiting. This is the Christ, the one whom God has sent to save us. How amazing to hold a baby in your arms and know that this is the one God is going to use to rescue many, who would otherwise be heading for eternal destruction. So now he speaks of the 'peace' of God: he has seen salvation from God; a great act of God for revelation to the nations and glory to Israel. He takes Mary aside, with another prophecy, wanting to say something which must have been harder for her to hear—that her son would be the cause of the falling and rising of many in Israel, and that her own soul would be 'pierced'. We may wonder at what she felt when she heard those words, containing as they did both prophecy of the amazing glory which her child Jesus was to reveal, but also of a work ahead of him which would involve great suffering—particularly for her, but also for other people who would, in some cases, fall, and whose hearts would be judged. But you get the sense with Simeon, as you hear more about him, that this is the moment he has been waiting for; that it defines the significance of his life, and that he would be happy to die now. When we read of Simeon praying about departing 'in peace', we know that he had now seen it all; he had great assurance that God was going to accomplish his purpose through this child. Some people's lives are like that: there is a particularly defining moment when God does a major thing through them; that is what they have been created for.

What, then, can we say about Simeon and Anna? The Bible calls people like them 'watchmen'. Like lookouts in the crow's nest at the top of a ship, who keep their eyes on the horizon, they were looking out for what God was going to do. People in the crow's nest can see further than others. In a film entitled *Longitude*, about establishing methods of working out longitude at sea, we learn that people tested out competing theories about how to discover where land might be. Eventually, the lookouts see land, and then one person's theory is vindicated, whilst another's is falsified. Those watching from the crow's nest are very important people, but they do not seem to do much; they are just up there! They are not engaged in working the ship, unlike the other crew members; but if they fail, like those on the Titanic who saw the iceberg only at the last moment, then the ship is obviously in great trouble. In spiritual terms, people in the crow's nest—God's watchmen—are the ones who are convinced that God is active in the world; that he is doing things and will go on doing great things; and they are waiting for what he will do next. They are alert people, and their alertness to God's fulfilment of his word is something every Christian can have; this is what God wants our prayer life to be like. Sometimes, when we pray, we may feel a sense of resignation (as when the lookout in the crow's nest starts to feel that he is never going to see land). At times like that, our praying is done by rote, and it all seems a bit of an effort. At other times, prayer life can be quite busy (like doing many things in the crow's nest except looking out): this is when you pray a lot of words, without really being alert to what God is saying. Our prayer lives may be continually interrupted.

How easy do you find it to set apart some time on your own when you can simply be with God, alert to him and to what the Holy Spirit may say to you? We get interrupted a good deal these days. The average British executive is said to receive 190 messages a day, including 48 phone calls, 38 emails, 20 letters, 13 post-it notes, 12 message slips, 11 voice mail messages, 11 faxes, 8 mobile phone calls, 3 express post deliveries, 2 pager messages and 3 courier deliveries. Four out of ten people are interrupted every ten minutes. Our lives are very rushed, and finding that time to be alone with God every day, ready and alert to him, is a vital thing that the account of Simeon and Anna can teach us.

They are also *prophetically gifted* people. Some in every congregation are like that; in certain ways, they can 'see' further than the rest. If God has gifted you in hearing the voice of the Spirit concerning what God is saying to us now, then you yourself are a gift to the Church. I encourage you to stay focused on listening to God and on being attentive to him, and if you feel there is something he is saying to your church, or to particular people, you should say those things at an appropriate time, exercising wisdom in the way you do so; and have the humility to accept that what you hear needs to be appropriately tested.

We are not all called to be prophets like Simeon and Anna, though we should heed Paul's encouragement to 'eagerly desire' spiritual gifts, especially the gift of prophecy. (See I Cor.14:1.) But if we sit back, hoping that things will just turn up, without being alert to God's voice and to his activity in our midst, then we are not going to be ready to co-operate in whatever he wants to do. *Attentiveness to God's Word and Spirit* is one essential feature of the effective Christian life, which Simeon and Anna display, and another is that they were under the leading of God himself; Simeon was moved by the Holy Spirit to go to the Temple, and he had the tremendous faith and humility needed to wait for God's moment. When you are waiting like that, you cannot force things to happen. *We need to allow God to direct our lives.*

Above all, we remember that Simeon and Anna were *in the Spirit.* We, too, need the indwelling Holy Spirit to speak to us through the Scriptures and in prayer, to give us the power to tell other people about Jesus effectively. As we live under God's authority, opening ourselves to receive with thankfulness more of the love and power of his Holy Spirit, we can expect that he will do new things among us, enabling us to present the gospel to people who do not know him; bringing true hope to those who feel so hurt, broken and lost in the world today.

*Heavenly Father, as you revealed to Simeon who Jesus is; help me to recognise Jesus, too. Enable me to see what you are doing, and to hear what you are saying to me.*

*Give me a heart for worship of you, and a readiness to speak of your redemption, as Anna did.*

# 2

# Identification: John the Baptist

*Patrick Whitworth*

---

'Identification' or 'identity' is a central issue in the Gospels. The question is, of course: 'who is Jesus?' It is an age-old question, but one which Jesus himself pressed home amongst the disciples, asking them, "But who do you say that I am?" It is, in fact, a question which a vast number of people rarely really answer. The matter of identity and identification lies at the heart of the meeting with Jesus which we are considering here:

> The next day John saw Jesus coming toward him and said, "Look, the Lamb of God, who takes away the sin of the world! This is the one I meant when I said, 'A man who comes after me has surpassed me because he was before me.' I myself did not know him, but the reason I came baptizing with water was that he might be revealed to Israel."
> Then John gave this testimony: "I saw the Spirit come down from heaven as a dove and remain on him. I would not have known him, except that the one who sent me to baptize with water told me, 'The man on whom you see the Spirit come down and remain is he who will baptize with the Holy Spirit.' I have seen and I testify that this is the Son of God."
>
> *John 1:29–34*

It is possible that Jesus and John had met before. They were cousins (see Luke 1:36) related on their mothers' side of the family. We know from Luke's account that Mary and Elizabeth, their respective mothers, met during their pregnancies. (See Luke1:41.)

19

John had reacted in that prenatal meeting by leaping for joy in his mother's womb! It is possible to imagine Elizabeth and Mary meeting with their children subsequently and talking, as mothers do, of their hopes for them; and, in their case, they had special reasons to do so. At the very least, John must have heard his mother speak often of Mary and Jesus, and would have been acquainted with some of the stories and facts that circulated, concerning Jesus' birth.

However, John had followed his own Spirit-compelled vocation as he grew up. The circumstances of his own birth propelled him in an unusual direction. (See Luke 1:5–25.) In the tradition of Samuel in the Old Testament, John was dedicated to God's service from birth. Prophecy had surrounded both his conception and arrival; he would bring back many people to the Lord their God. Indeed, John stands in a remarkable way as the bridge between the old and new testaments. At the end of the Old Testament Malachi prophesies that God will send, '...the prophet Elijah before that great and dreadful day of the LORD comes. He will turn the hearts of the fathers to their children, and the hearts of the children to their fathers....' (See Malachi 4:6.) At the outset of the New Testament, the angel of the Lord prophesies that John will, "...go on before the Lord, in the spirit and power of Elijah, to turn the hearts of the fathers to their children..." (Luke 1:17). But, at root, John's vocation was to prepare the people for their Messiah.

Prior to his climactic meeting with Jesus, John had already spent some time in the desert. His lifestyle both attracted and held the people. His clothing was rudimentary and ascetic; his diet, to say the least, unusual.

So great was the stir created by John's message and call to repentance and baptism, that a kind of commission of enquiry was sent down to investigate his activity in the desert regions of the Jordan river. (See John 1:19–28.) The question they had come to ask was essentially 'who are you?' Once again, we are faced with the issue of identity. It appears that this delegation of Levites and priests had three categories into which John might fit. Was he the Christ? No. Was he Elijah? Here they were closer to the mark, for although he was not Elijah himself, John was very much like Elijah and Jesus later confirmed this to the crowds. (See Matthew 11:14.) But John denied that he was Elijah himself, or indeed the other prophet to whom the enquirers alluded. John's sparse response to their enquiry was that his was a voice of one calling in the desert,

'Prepare the way for the Lord, make straight paths for him' —and that it was time for all Israel to repent.

If the issue of John's identity was important to the rulers of Israel because they needed to know who he was before they could either approve or condemn him, the issue of who Jesus was became far more important. The Jewish leaders were always ambivalent about John, because they knew that if they agreed that he had been sent by God then the next question would focus on why had they not believed his message, been baptised, and believed in the Messiah whom he came to identify. Again and again, Jesus would expose their ambivalence toward John. (See Matthew 21:25.) In the end, events overtook them all; John was beheaded as a result of a rash promise by King Herod the Tetrarch to Salome, who in turn had agreed to her mother's request that John be beheaded for criticising her marriage.

But, as we have seen, the issue of John's identity was always intimately intertwined with Jesus, because John unambiguously announced, to all who would hear, the identity of Jesus and what he had come to do. This momentous declaration took place by the Jordan, at the water's edge. In the course of just a few sentences, an amazing identification took place. According to John the apostle and evangelist, on the very next day, following the commission of enquiry from Jerusalem to investigate John, Jesus arrived at the place where John was baptising. Jesus approached John, who was presumably baptising at the time. Using words which were in keeping with John's simple lifestyle, he announced the Messiah to an expectant and waiting world: "Look, the Lamb of God, who takes away the sin of the world!" This declaration made some extremely profound statements about what Jesus would do and who he was.

In identifying Jesus as the Lamb of God who takes away the sin of the world, John pre-eminently acknowledged that Jesus was God's provision for human sin and moral failure. Above all else, he had come to deal with sin by becoming a sacrifice—an atonement for it. He would become in his death like a sacrificial lamb; so that, through faith in this death, we might have the guilt and effect of failure removed. As John declared by his announcement, this would be Jesus' greatest action. He would have the authority and power to remove, or take away, the sin of the world.

Let me make this huge doctrinal statement a little more understandable. We are all used to rubbish disposal. There is rubbish to be collected from our home, as with all households. Each day, a little is taken from the kitchen to the bins outside the house. Once a week, the local authority send their refuse collectors round to our streets to collect it all. Thankfully, they are very regular in their collection, otherwise the refuse would spill over the bins—there would be a stench in the summer, and maggots would take up residence. If, for any reason, it were not collected, we would ring up the waste department of our council. However, there is one small task that we must do: to put the bins at the end of our driveway so that they can be seen and all that nasty stuff can be taken away. You see the point. Jesus entered the world to take away our human moral waste; it cost him the sacrifice of his life, as though he was a sacrificial lamb, but it is our duty to put out the waste so that he can take it away. Putting out the rubbish both acknowledges that it *is* rubbish and that it *does* need collecting, otherwise it will only fester, becoming in time a risk to our health.

In moral terms, surely, we know what constitutes rubbish: bitterness, hatred, envy, lust, to mention only a few items of refuse —yet we persist in thinking either that it can be used as food or that it does not pose a health risk if we let it linger in our lives. As he announced Jesus as the Messiah, John identified him as the great 'rubbish collector' —but this offer to collect our moral refuse took Jesus to death on the cross. As Jesus is the eternal Son of God he can continue to collect our moral rubbish for ever.

The second thing that John says Jesus will do is to immerse his people in the Spirit. 'The man on whom you see the Spirit come down and remain is he who will baptise with the Holy Spirit', God said to John in a moment of special revelation at the river Jordan. So not only does Jesus 'take away' but also he 'baptises' (immerses) people in the Holy Spirit. The double action of Jesus is, on the one hand, to remove our moral guilt and, on the other, to fill the individual with the fullness of the Spirit. Once again, this is an *eternal* action of the Son: he goes on immersing us with the Holy Spirit, who had come upon him as a dove in the river Jordan.

Another picture might bring home the reality of this statement of John. Imagine that it is a hot summer day and children have been playing in your garden. They are hot, thirsty, dirty and tired. What will revive them? You have an idea; you go to fetch the garden hose, attach it to an outdoor tap, and turn the cool, cascading water on the squealing children. They love it—running in and out of the water until they are completely drenched. They are now cool, clean, refreshed; and their thirst is met by gulping the torrent of water as it passes over them. In a way you could say that they were 'immersed'. This is an apt picture of what Jesus will do when he baptises the people of God with the Spirit, except that not only does this immersion refresh but, more importantly, it takes us into God's life and kingdom, equipping and empowering us for mission.

An example of this happening in an individual's life occurred when I offered to pray for a man in his forties who had come to the front of the church for prayer, at the end of a service. He was weeping copiously, and was embarrassed by this as it was unusual for him. He had recently come back to God. I asked him whether anything was amiss. "No," he replied. In fact he was wonderfully happy; the action of the Spirit in his life was to bring a profusion of tears, and he did not know what was going on. I told him that in the Orthodox Church tears were often seen as an accompaniment to the Spirit's work. He was being *immersed* in the Spirit by the same Christ who had himself been immeasurably filled with the Spirit whilst he was baptised by John in the river Jordan. I went on to explain that it had been known for some people to weep under the Spirit's power for days—I am not sure how reassuring he found that!

So, in this brief encounter with Jesus, John declares that the man coming towards him was the one who would do two things: he would take away sin and he would immerse in the Holy Spirit those from whom he had previously collected their moral refuse.

Having told his hearers what Jesus would do, John now identified him in what seems to have been unmistakeable terms. He made two remarkable statements about Jesus' identity in the course of his testimony or declaration by the Jordan. Firstly, he said: "This is the one I meant when I said, 'A man who comes after me has surpassed me because he was before me'" (John 1:30). John's final phrase in this statement is curious, making the hearer ask himself, 'What does John mean by saying that Jesus was before him?' Further enquiry of the Greek for 'before me' throws up the word 'protos', from which we derive such words as 'prototype', which is a clue to the essence of John's meaning here. What John is saying is that in Jesus we have the one who is 'first' in terms both of status and existence. As the apostle John has already told us in his prologue, Jesus as the Word was, 'in the beginning', and was before all things, and so certainly was 'before' John the Baptist.

But, more than this, John is also indicating that Jesus is the model man, the prototype of the 'new man' whom Paul also describes in Romans 4. Indeed, John the Baptist and Pilate concur that Jesus is THE MAN; as Pilate famously announced Jesus to the crowd in Jerusalem with the words, "Ecce Homo". (See John 19:5.) So in a moment of divinely inspired insight, John teaches that Jesus is the prototype of the human race, the model of our humanity.

Secondly, John makes an even more unmistakeable statement about the identity of Jesus. He concludes his testimony to the crowds with this announcement: "I have seen and I testify that this is the Son of God" (John 1:34). Here is a striking admission of faith. Considering that it took some of the disciples three years of being in the presence of Jesus, witnessing his miracles and teaching, seeing his death, and meeting him in his resurrected body, before many of them believed what John said about him at his first meeting, John's confession of faith anticipates in a most astonishing way what was still to take place. The reason for this perception is also here in this passage. It appears that, as Jesus was approaching John, God the Father was speaking directly to John the Baptist, so that he was able to identify Jesus as the Son of God. John says, quite honestly and humbly, "I would not have known him, except that the one who sent me to baptize with water told me..." (John 1:33).

John had identified Jesus as the Son of God, the one who was 'first', and in so doing blazes a trail for others to follow in the Gospels. We shall watch many others come and wrestle with this question: 'who is Jesus?' I invite you to take a moment now to answer this question. Who do *you* say that Jesus is? And if you recognise his authority, have you allowed him to remove whatever rubbish clutters your life, and to immerse you in the Holy Spirit who came upon him as a dove at his baptism?

*Lord Jesus, help me to know who you are and to recognise you, as John did. Open my ears, that I may hear you speak to me, as John heard the Father speak to him that day by the Jordan. Please collect the rubbish of my life and, in particular, these things....*

*Please come and immerse me in the Holy Spirit, who came upon you at your baptism, so that I may know your life and power. Thank you that you became the sacrifice for my failures; draw me close to your heart today. Amen.*

# 3

# Temptation:
# The Devil

## Patrick Whitworth

It is quite reasonable to argue that this 'meeting' was not one in the ordinary sense of that word. In our series of meetings, this is very much the 'odd one out', involving, as it does, an encounter between Jesus and a non-human entity—a fallen angelic power. We cannot be sure in what form this encounter took place, but we are amply justified in including it, for it was a real meeting, of which Jesus must have told his disciples, and three of the evangelists include the account in their Gospels.

> Jesus, full of the Holy Spirit, returned from the Jordan and was led by the Spirit in the desert, where for forty days he was tempted by the devil. He ate nothing during those days, and at the end of them he was hungry.
>
> The devil said to him, "If you are the Son of God, tell this stone to become bread."
>
> Jesus answered, "It is written: 'Man does not live on bread alone.'"
>
> The devil led him up to a high place and showed him in an instant all the kingdoms of the world. And he said to him, "I will give you all their authority and splendour, for it has been given to me, and I can give it to anyone I want to. So if you worship me, it will all be yours."
>
> Jesus answered, "It is written: 'Worship the Lord your God and serve him only.'"
>
> The devil led him to Jerusalem, and had him stand on the highest point of the temple. "If you are the Son of God," he said, "throw yourself down from here. For it is written:

'He will command his angels concerning you, to guard you carefully; they will lift you up in their hands, so that you will not strike your foot against a stone.'"

Jesus answered, "It says, 'Do not put the Lord your God to the test.'"

When the devil had finished all this tempting, he left him until an opportune time.

*Luke 4:1–13*

Although many people today have difficulty in believing in the existence of a personal devil, Jesus had no such problem. He did not have an encounter with a figment of his imagination, but with one who was all too real, and of whom Jesus spoke in clear terms on a number of occasions. In the heat of a fierce argument with the Jewish leaders, Jesus said to them, "You belong to your father, the devil, and you want to carry out your father's desire. He was a murderer from the beginning, not holding to the truth, for there is no truth in him. When he lies, he speaks his native language, for he is a liar and the father of lies" (John 8:44). You could not get more explicit than that and, as always with Jesus' teaching, you have a stark choice either to accept what he says or maintain that he was gravely mistaken, deceived or bordering on lunacy. But if we, like John the Baptist, have already accepted him as the Son of God, then we are not free to 'pick and mix' his teaching. Jesus knew whom he was encountering in the desert, and he was under no illusion. Nor did the devil try to disguise himself: his assault on Jesus was head-on, even if at times the actual temptation was cleverly disguised.

Before considering the substance of their dialogue, we must answer the question, 'why did this meeting occur at this point—at the very beginning of Jesus' ministry?' In Luke's narrative, the temptations take place after the baptism of Jesus, his filling with the Spirit and the establishment of his human identity with a long list of names which display his genealogy on Joseph's side, but from whom, in fact, he was not 'genetically' descended. Luke, like Matthew, is establishing the pedigree of Jesus' lineage, showing how his descent fulfilled Old Testament prophecy that the Messiah would be descended from David. So by the time Luke comes to tell us of the temptations of Jesus, he has already shown us both his human and his divine origin. The Father's voice has declared at Jesus' baptism, "You are my Son, whom I love; with you I am well pleased." Assured of his identity, both human and divine; assured of the Father's love and commitment to him; filled with

26

the Holy Spirit and, incidentally, Luke tells us, about thirty years old, Jesus is literally kicked out by the Spirit into the desert. He is taken, under the guidance of the Spirit, from the very pinnacle of assurance to another—quite different—pinnacle of temptation; why is this?

Temptation can be defined as an allurement or opportunity to sin or break a moral command, and can sometimes signify 'testing' or 'trial'. Temptations can vary in seriousness from the proverbial cream-cake-too-far to robbing a bank because you are short of cash, and anything in between. Temptations are incitements to sin proceeding from the world, the flesh or the devil. In slight contrast, 'trial' may mean a set of circumstances you find yourself in, which constitute a period of severe testing of your faith or trust in God. Of course, both may be present together. Jesus suffered both trial and temptation in acute form over a period of time, which could better be described as spiritual struggle, or warfare of the most intense kind. If this was the sort of temptation Jesus faced, why did it happen?

In short, it was a testing of the purpose and attitude of the Son of God, which the Father allowed and the Spirit directed him into. The clues to the meaning and significance of this whole episode are best found in the letter to the Hebrews. The author of Hebrews gives both theological and psychological insight into Jesus' life and ministry. He tells us that, 'During the days of Jesus' life on earth, he offered up prayers and petitions with loud cries and tears to the one who could save him from death, and he was heard because of his reverent submission' (Hebrews 5:7). Surely, some of those days of anguished petition fell within the forty days of temptation in the wilderness of Judea? During the course of those days he was being severely tested, and so prepared for the ministry and conflict that lay ahead—nor is this at all surprising.

In the last chapter, we noticed that John the Baptist hailed Jesus as the first or the 'protos', and we thought of Jesus being the 'new man' or the prototype of the new race, about which Paul so eloquently speaks in his letter to the Ephesians. Paul teaches them that God's purpose was to create, through Jesus' death on the cross, in Christ, one **new man** out of the two (Gentile and Jew). What do you do with prototypes, but test them! So Jesus, the new Man, the prototype of this new race, is tested severely, both to prepare him and to help his people.

I read of a young British runner who is a marathon hopeful.

Following a few emails to the world's leading marathon runner and his wife (from Morocco), they agreed to take him on and train him. He was flown to New Mexico and trained arduously for three weeks. At the end, the trainer said of this young hopeful, "...He was training with us for three weeks and he went through hell, but he did not miss any work outs. Sometimes I said to him, 'If you feel you cannot do this training, we can do it tomorrow', but he would always do it."

Jesus had more than a marathon to run, and his testing and training included physical hardship, a forty day fast, and spiritual trial and temptation. The purpose of this testing was not only to prepare him for what lay ahead but also to help us, so that in *our* prayers for help in time of trial and temptation we can go to Jesus. In the words of the writer to the Hebrews, 'For we do not have a high priest who is unable to sympathize with our weaknesses, but we have one who has been tempted in every way, just as we are— yet was without sin' (Hebrews 4:15). It is now time to consider in more detail the particular temptations that Jesus faced and how his victory in this desert campaign helps us.

The first temptation Jesus faced from the devil was an attempt to hit Jesus where he was most vulnerable: a common ploy in the devil's book of tactics. As we know, Jesus had been fasting for forty days which, on any calculation, is a very long time. A single twenty four hour fast is hard enough! In a typical piece of understatement by Doctor Luke, recounting the physical deprivations of Jesus he simply says that 'he was hungry.'

So with acute subtlety the devil tempts Jesus to turn some desert stone lying on the ground into a loaf of bread that would be warm, fresh and delicious. So, you ask, why was this such a dangerous temptation for Jesus? It was for a number of reasons. Firstly, if Jesus did it the motive for the action would have been doubly wrong. The first wrong motive would have been attempting to demonstrate to the devil that he really was the Son of God, which the devil had called into question with the preface to his request— "If you are the Son of God...." Jesus was not in the business of proving who he was by party tricks. Later in the same Gospel, Jesus was hauled up before Herod the Tetrarch, who had rashly allowed John the Baptist to be beheaded, and refused him a performance miracle which we are told he had hoped to see (Luke 23:8). So Jesus refused to fall into the trap of proving who he was by a knock-down miracle. The second wrong motive for such an action was that he would have been performing the miracle to satisfy his own great hunger. In fact, to have done what the devil requested would have involved an abuse of the gift of power with which Jesus had been entrusted following his baptism and reception of the Spirit's power. Now we are on firmer ground. All of us are familiar with the temptation to abuse power. Perhaps it is one of the commonest and worst abuses that there is.

I am writing this after a large number of bodies have been found in buildings in South West Uganda due to some cult leaders persuading these people to take their own lives or forcing them to do so—an abuse of power on a terrible scale. I am writing this in an area of the British Isles where there has been systematic abuse of children in children's homes—a dreadful abuse of power. Many of us exercise power, which in biblical terms is always a gift of God for which we shall be held accountable, as parents, teachers, clergy, employers, managers, politicians and so on, and we are to exercise it in the way that Jesus did. He did not use it for his own ends, to satisfy his own hunger or to proclaim his own identity. He used it to speak the words of the Father, to do the works of the Father and to fulfil his own vocation, which took him to the cross and beyond. So Jesus turned down the devil's request that he provide himself with a 'take-away'; instead he gave us an answer that has become proverbial. Quoting from Deuteronomy, Jesus said: "Man does not live on bread alone." From Matthew's account, we learn that Jesus added, "...but on every word that comes from the mouth of God" (Matthew 4:4). By using this quotation, not only does Jesus deflect the assault of the devil upon him but also establishes a vital point about his own needs. Jesus is saying that despite needing food he also needed the sustenance of doing his Father's will.

The same point is made by Jesus when talking to the disciples in John 4. When they return from some shopping in Sychar, they find him in conversation with the notorious Samaritan woman and, no doubt having themselves eaten, urge him to eat too. Jesus responds to their urgings by saying, "I have food to eat that you know nothing about." The disciples, who are often confused by Jesus' catering arrangements, wonder whether he has a secret supplier, so he explains what he meant: "My food...is to do the will of him who sent me and to finish his work." Here, surely, is the meaning behind his earlier rebuttal of the devil: he finds both a form of sustenance and nourishment in doing the Father's will. As his life and ministry were founded upon this principle of doing the will of the Father, he was well able to resist the devil's temptation of making him misuse his power to provide bread that he had decided to forgo.

If the first temptation was to misuse his power, the second was for Jesus to misdirect his worship. I find the second temptation so blatant and frontal in its assault upon the integrity of Jesus that it beggars belief. The occasion of the temptation was some form of vision. It involved Jesus being taken to some high mountain from where, in an instant, Jesus could see all the kingdoms of the world. The only place from which this is literally physically possible is outer space, hence the idea of a vision. If this temptation shows anything about the devil's tactics it is that he will stop at nothing. Presumably the temptation is founded upon the principle, which is almost universally true, that everyone has their price. As far as the devil was concerned it was simply a very high one! Once again there are, in this temptation, underlying issues of authority or power. For Jesus there appear to have been two ways to power: either this simple act of allegiance to, and worship of, the devil, or obedience to the Father's will and purpose for him, which ultimately led through the cross to triumph and exaltation. Of course we know the way Jesus chose, which resulted in him saying at the end of the Gospel of Matthew, "All authority in heaven and on earth has been given to me." As a result of his obedience, he received from his Father all authority in heaven and earth.

But the devil, in this second temptation, had presented him with the starkest of choices. Jesus, once again, had rebutted the enemy's words with a quotation from elsewhere in Deuteronomy, in which he recalled the fundamental teaching that Moses had given to the Israelites. At its heart this teaching contained the commandment to worship the Lord only. The quotation went on to say, 'Do not follow other gods, the gods of the peoples around you...' (Deuteronomy 6:14).

This brutal, aggressive temptation that Jesus faced in the desert is one we all face in either subtler or more insidious ways. In our secular and consumerist society, the temptation is to give our allegiance, devotion and worship to the 'gods' of the people we live amongst. They are not hard to identify; very often they are objects—in the gleaming car salesroom, on the internet, in the boardroom; or they are thrills and pleasures on the terraces, in the bedroom, through a joyride, in the gym. We live for the next time, the next pleasure, and we give to them our devotion, our allegiance: yes, our worship. These temptations may not be overcome at a stroke, as appeared to be the case for Jesus in the desert. For most of us it is an ongoing campaign; but to fight it we must have the same determination as Jesus to, 'worship the Lord your God and serve him only', and continually to call upon the aid of the Spirit who so filled Jesus.

The third temptation Jesus faced was in the city, in Jerusalem. Again, it presumably took place in some visionary form, but was nonetheless real. If the first temptation was for Jesus to misuse his power and the second to misdirect his worship, the third was to mistake his vocation. Once again, Jesus is taken to a high point, in fact the highest in Jerusalem: the pinnacle of the Temple. Built by Herod the Great and only recently completed, it was the centre of the Jewish religion. It represented the centre of the power structure arraigned against Jesus, and underlying both his teaching and his actions was a challenge to the Jewish people to choose between him and that establishment. We see this clearly in the meeting Jesus had with the high priest during his trial. But, for now, the Temple is the scene for his third temptation. Jesus is taken to its highest point and encouraged to throw himself down on the understanding that his Father will turn his fall into a remarkable bungee jump, whereby the angels will gather him up before he hits the ground. Again, it is an astonishing temptation. However, the kernel of it was that, through this miracle, Jesus should take the fast route to fame and so become the toast of the people. It says more about the devil's understanding of glory than anything else.

Within this temptation, however, lies a serious challenge to Jesus' integrity. It presented Jesus with a kind of choice. The devil rightly perceived that Jesus expected to become the leader of his people. However, the devil had little or no idea of how it would come about. Indeed, people become leaders in various ways. It can be through the ballot box; it can be through revolution and the gun. It may be through largesse and, in a religious society, it can be through a sign that says that you have been sent by God. All Jesus' contemporaries misunderstood how he would become the leader of his people; even his disciples thought that he would become king and overthrow the Romans. We might reasonably presume that the devil thought that he would become leader by means of an act which would lead to fame.

The devil had become a little more subtle than in the previous temptation. As in the first temptation, the devil was urging Jesus to prove that he was the Son of God, in this case by a spectacular jump and rescue operation that would be witnessed by the crowds below. In this way he would prove himself God's Son (although Jesus knew that they would take more convincing) and hopefully become, as a result, the leader of the Jewish people. To encourage Jesus to perform this feat, the devil wrapped up the idea in Scripture. But Jesus saw how this temptation would fatally flaw his mission; it would totally undermine his vocation. His vocation was not to win the love and allegiance of the people by this absurd act based on misapplied scripture; his vocation was to go to the cross whereby he would save people from their sins. Jumping off roofs, however high, was not part of his vocation! He would save his people not by an act of 'fame' but through his death on the cross.

So Jesus resisted the devil, replying with another quotation from Deuteronomy, on the narrow grounds of not putting to the test the Lord your God. He did not inform the devil as to how he would become the leader of the people through the plan of the cross; you do not discuss your battle plan with your enemy. But Jesus knew, even then, that the feat he was called to was, 'to give his life as a ransom for many', and the angels would witness the Father through the Spirit raising him to new life.

Nor is this temptation wholly strange to us. Imagine a young actress making her way in the profession. She plans to work hard in repertory theatre, taking parts that show off her skills. Then she is noticed by a director who has cornered a less healthy end of the entertainment business. She is offered a part that will pay well, it will lead to better remunerated work, she will make a name for herself, but will completely compromise her integrity. She is told it will be a pathway to success. Often we face the temptation to compromise our integrity, to mistake our vocation, to settle for less than God's purpose for our life, and this temptation is made doubly hard when on the face of it God's vision for our life involves hardship and the other way appears easy.

At the end of this period of intense trial, temptation and proving, we are told by Luke that the devil left him, 'until a more opportune time', generally thought to have been the time of anguished prayer in Gethsemane; again, a time when Jesus was at his most vulnerable. Mark and Matthew tell us that, at the end of his temptations, angels came to minister to him, presumably strengthening him physically and encouraging him with their presence. What had Jesus achieved? The Scriptures provide their own commentary upon Jesus' triumph over this spiritual and physical assault. The writer to the Hebrews tells us that, 'Because he himself suffered when he was tempted, he is able to help those who are being tempted' (Hebrews 2:18). Jesus helps us by his example and by his power. His example shows how he withstood this assault; it was by a combination of word, Spirit and self-understanding. Undoubtedly, the bulwark of his defence was his understanding of the Scriptures: from him came not just a recitation of the verses, but an understanding that these scriptures expressed all that he wanted to say and be; so there was no division or chink between his desires and their teaching. At the same time, as we saw earlier, he came to his time of trial full of the Spirit, and he left this time of testing, also, in the power of the Spirit. As Luke says, 'Jesus returned to Galilee in the power of the Spirit', so we learn from Jesus' example a healthy and vital dependence on the Spirit, in facing temptations of all kinds. Finally, we see from Jesus' example a complete self-awareness. He knew what his Father's will for him was, and in the certainty of that knowledge he was able to rebut the devil's words and resist his schemes.

However, the example of Jesus could daunt us by its perfection; our poor knowledge of the Scriptures, our leaky spiritual cisterns and our faulty self understanding, could leave us overwhelmed. But he has left open another way, as expressed by the writer to the Hebrews, namely the avenue of prayer, by which we may find help in times of testing, trial or temptation. It is through prayer, and through the work of the Holy Spirit, that in moments of temptation, in periods of trial, or in facing sorrows of the heart, we receive that promised help.

*Lord Jesus help me to follow your good example; to use the gifts and influence you have given me, so that neither you nor I need be ashamed; help me to direct my worship only to you and turn my back on those things or experiences that want my devotion. Help me to fulfil the calling that you have given me, and not to journey by some other route. Help me to use the weapons you wielded well: your word, the Spirit and right knowledge of myself. Above all, in my trials may I learn to come to you for help. Amen.*

# 4

# Vocation:
# Simon Peter

## *Patrick Whitworth*

---

The foundations of Jesus' ministry in the Gospels are laid around a number of events: his baptism by John the Baptist together with the empowering by the Spirit; his temptations in the wilderness; and the calling of the disciples.

In his Gospel, John tells us that Andrew heard John the Baptist speaking about Jesus, and so started following him. Andrew then found his brother, Simon Peter, and brought him to Jesus. Later, Philip and Nathanael joined the company. Nathanael was especially impressed that Jesus knew both his name and whereabouts earlier that day (sitting under a fig-tree) without being told! Jesus said that he would see more marvellous things than that, if he joined their party. Later, James and John, the sons of Zebedee, would join the band of disciples. But it was the call of Simon Peter which is the classic of its kind, enshrining as it did all the vital features of a leader's call such as we see in the Old Testament, but now in the context of Jesus' inauguration of the kingdom of God. There is something especially exciting about Peter's call, coming as it does at the beginning of a new movement encapsulated in the phrase 'the kingdom of God'. The word 'kingdom' might suggest a political metaphor, but if we think of the feelings and hopes that surround the beginning of a new political administration or government, in our experience, the 'promise' is often not realised. The tremendous promise of the creator God, as he extends his dominion is, of course, unique, and does not disappoint. This is Luke's account of the call of Simon Peter.

> One day as Jesus was standing by the Lake of Gennesaret, with the people crowding around him and listening to the word of God, he saw at the water's edge two boats, left there by the fishermen, who were washing their nets. He got into one of the boats, the one belonging to Simon, and asked him to put out a little from the shore. Then he sat down and taught the people from the boat.
>
> When he had finished speaking, he said to Simon, "Put out into deep water, and let down the nets for a catch."
>
> Simon answered, "Master, we've worked hard all night and haven't caught anything. But because you say so, I will let down the nets."
>
> When they had done so, they caught such a large number of fish that their nets began to break. So they signalled their partners in the other boat to come and help them, and they came and filled both boats so full that they began to sink.
>
> When Simon Peter saw this, he fell at Jesus' knees and said, "Go away from me, Lord; I am a sinful man!" For he and all his companions were astonished at the catch of fish they had taken, and so were James and John, the sons of Zebedee, Simon's partners.
>
> Then Jesus said to Simon, "Don't be afraid; from now on you will catch men." So they pulled their boats up on shore, left everything and followed him.
>
> *Luke 5:1–11*

We see a process beginning here, a world-changing plan worked out, as Jesus calls and gathers together the disciples, a small group he was to teach the ways of God and train for ministry in the kingdom. These disciples, who were to share his life, often made mistakes and let him down. Jesus showed them the love of God, forgiving and correcting when necessary. They were to be dynamically used by God, and later, when they received a new empowering from the Holy Spirit, their impact on countless other people was to be truly phenomenal.

There are many examples of God's call of leaders in the Old Testament, which we could compare with Simon Peter's call, but probably the ones to hold in mind are those of Abraham, Jacob, Moses, Samuel and the prophets, especially Isaiah, Jeremiah and Ezekiel, for there are marked similarities between their vocations and Simon Peter's. As we look at the main features of his call, we will briefly compare it with theirs. However, what we can be sure of is, that to a greater or lesser extent, these same features will be present in the call of any disciple who follows Jesus today, and especially anyone called to serve God as a leader of others.

There are several aspects of Simon's vocation to highlight. They are: a revelation of God's glory; a response of inadequacy; a reiteration of promise, a change of name and a simultaneous call both to leave and cleave. We will explore each of these in turn.

## A REVELATION OF GOD'S GLORY

Jesus had been teaching the people from Simon's boat, which gave him a seat from which to instruct the people and also afforded a little 'crowd control', as he was able to push out from the shore and thereby gain some space from the edge of the throng. Seated in the boat, presumably with Simon aboard to hold it steady, Jesus taught the people. When he had finished, Jesus embarked on the other main piece of work to be done that day—the call of Simon. It is quite clear that Jesus had known Simon for a while. Though it is often difficult to work out the exact chronology of the Gospels, Simon would have had ample time to watch Jesus in action before this incident. So he would have had some time to begin to evaluate who Jesus was, even if, as yet, he had no fully formed opinion of his status. Jesus suggested a fishing trip, knowing well that Peter had already had a fruitless night of fishing. In telling Simon to put out into deep water, and let down his nets for a catch, Jesus was not suggesting a bit of hand lining over the back for amusement's sake, but a full scale piece of fishing in deep water, involving a sail or row to get to the fishing grounds, and the deployment of all the boat's nets. It involved work, but it was also serious and expectant action. Understandably, Simon objected, but was willing to trust the word of Jesus: a vital step of faith for him and for all Christians in every age, including our own.

The outcome was overwhelming for Simon, for the boats which began to sink with the weight of the fish, and for James and John, his fishing partners, too. We may assume that never before on Galilee had so many fish been caught by so few fishermen in such a short time! For Simon it was, as it was meant to be, an awesome moment—he saw a miracle occur before his eyes, as ordinary fishing was overtaken by a huge catch; this was a moment when something of the transcendent glory of God was disclosed to him. We may be confident that this was the way Simon saw it, because of his reaction.

## A RESPONSE OF INADEQUACY

When Simon had taken in what had happened, and put two and two together, he acknowledged his own sinfulness and asked Jesus, therefore, to depart from him. There is no doubt that he understood the event as God-given! He did not think that they had run into a huge shoal of fish by some mere accident. In this more domestic setting it was, nonetheless, a disclosure of God's power and authority at work in Jesus, indicating divine generosity and the outcome of obedience to his word; what Simon had to puzzle out for some time longer was how Jesus related to God. Later, he would come to his own unambiguous confession that Jesus was 'the Christ, the Son of the living God', and that confession would be tested by fire. Understanding now that this catch signified a glorious moment of revelation, Simon realised that he was in the presence of God's holy love; and like so many others before and since, his reaction makes it clear that he felt unworthy and unready for this moment. In asking Jesus to depart from him, Simon was in good company. Most of the great leaders in the Old Testament felt the same way when they were called to represent God. Moses pleaded with God that he was a man of few words and could not speak before Pharaoh. Isaiah said that he was 'a man of unclean lips', presumably thinking that this would disqualify him from God's service. Jeremiah said that he was too young to become a prophet, and Gideon hid from the very people God was asking him to overthrow, as they were oppressing the Israelites. The fact is that our imperfections are not a disqualification from God's service but a means whereby we become more dependent on him for the qualifying grace that he so generously gives. In fact, it is far healthier to feel acutely our own weakness, and to say so, than to think that we are up to the job.

I well remember being ordained at the age of twenty five to serve in a church with a considerable reputation in the North of England, that had a congregation of some seven hundred, which in UK terms is quite large, and feeling totally inadequate for the task. The kindly Bishop of Selby wrote to me at my ordination an encouraging note saying, 'It is wonderful to arrive at the great time (of ordination) after the training is finished, but perhaps for the first time you may feel a little diffident and inadequate at such a time. This itself is a blessing for it means that we can only throw ourselves entirely on the mercy and grace of God: "My grace is sufficient for thee, for my power is made perfect in weakness.'" I hasten to add it was not the first or last time of feeling more than inadequate for the task! Simon felt thoroughly unprepared for whatever lay ahead of him, and out of his depth. He thought he knew about fishing, but clearly Jesus knew more and could run the most successful fishing business on Galilee if he wished to! So Simon protested his inadequacy and, in doing so, qualified himself as a potential disciple—a new life for him, which was to turn out to be a 'roller coaster'. Nor was it the last time that he would receive from Jesus instructions on fishing!

## A REITERATION OF PROMISE

God's call to follow his Son and, in particular, his call to leadership is accompanied by a promise. To all his disciples, Jesus promises eternal life but, in addition, special promises were made to particular individuals when they were called, to encourage them to play their part in God's overall plan. This was true for Simon. Jesus told him not to be afraid. Fear often attends supernatural events and Jesus sought now to allay it. From then on, Simon's 'catch' would consist of people—a promise from Jesus that the fishermen could understand only dimly at that moment. Perhaps, when Jesus said this to Simon and his fishing partners, they were still looking at the moving mass of fish that filled their boats. In retrospect we understand what Jesus meant, namely that he would use the apostles, and indeed all his disciples, to bring others into his kingdom. The great catch of fish was a sign that what was possible with fish was possible with people, too.

As with many of the Old Testament leaders, Simon was given a promise at the outset of his discipleship. When God took Abraham outside his tent one clear night and asked him to look up at the stars, he made him a promise that one day his descendants would be as numerous as the stars in the sky. (See Genesis 15:5.) When God called Jeremiah to prophesy to the people of Judah about the coming judgment of the nation and the destruction of Jerusalem, unless they changed their ways, he also promised that he would rescue him (see Jeremiah 1:8) despite the obvious danger of this calling. Although one was a promise that took forward the purpose of God in an historic way, and the promise to Jeremiah was more a reassurance as to his personal safety during a tempestuous career as a prophet, both of these were promises given at the outset of their faith-journey. Simon was now given a promise, which was substantiated by the preceding miracle of the catch of fish, but the promise was not to find its fulfilment until the day of Pentecost. We may wonder whether Simon recalled the promise, and the miracle of the fish given by Jesus on the day of his call, at the address he gave on the day of Pentecost, when three thousand believed!

Since that day by Galilee, countless others have been called with a particular promise or, at their time of calling, have been given a particular vision. I have noticed in Africa that Christian leaders talk both of their call to discipleship and their 'missionary call' to a particular life's-work. Too often in the West we gladly accept our call to become a disciple without expecting that there will be a particular life-calling for us in line with our gifts. It is those who respond to this life call who often show the greatest evidence of maturity and effectiveness in their discipleship.

## A CALL TO LEAVE AND CLEAVE
The final part of Simon's call could not be more radical. We are told that the fishermen pulled their boats ashore, left everything, and followed Jesus. There may be a temptation to try to rationalize what took place, watering it down so that this sudden leaving is thought of as actually taking place over a period, so that proper management structures could be put in place for the fishing business. We might wonder what plans were made to take care of dependent relatives! However, the plain meaning of the text was that they did exactly what was recorded: they pulled up their boats, presumably arranged for the distribution or sale of the fish, then went off into the sunset with Jesus, deliriously happy! Why not? After all, theirs was a totally different lifestyle to ours. No need to inform the local council one would not be living at home for a while; no need to make advance payments for the mortgage; no need to arrange for gas, water, telephone and electricity to be discontinued. What could have been more exciting for a few young men in their late teens or early twenties: a cause; a leader; an adventure, and an uncertain conclusion! Whereas we in the West spend most of our waking hours squeezing risk out of our lives, Jesus offered it in platefuls to these young men. But this was to be no ordinary adventure! In ways they could not at that point have imagined, this was to be a world-changing venture of FAITH in him, and in the Holy Spirit's power, for the whole of their lives.

The dynamic that Simon and the other disciples were called to was 'leaving and cleaving', the same two principles that apply in marriage. It is clear that the disciples were called to leave homes, their local area, their livelihood, families and friends. It must have been a wrench and, from later conversations, we suspect that their motives may, in some cases, have been mixed. But they were not called merely to leave, they were called to *stay* with Jesus.

This is made abundantly clear in Mark's description of the appointment of the twelve apostles, a formal act in which Jesus commissioned them as his principal disciples and future leaders of the Church, although one would be lost. In the summary, Mark tells us that the twelve were appointed to 'preach and to have authority to drive out demons', but also simply to be 'with him'. (See Mark 3:13–15.) This sets the pattern for all discipleship: *coming* to be with Jesus in prayer, listening, learning and observing; and *going* out to speak, heal, deliver and bring the Lord's peace. It is in this 'coming' and 'going' that all discipleship takes place. Simon was to have plenty of experience in the future as to what this meant and how it could be worked out in his life.

## A CHANGE OF NAME

Although Luke does not in his account tell us of Simon's change of name, it appears in John's record of Simon's call: 'And he [Andrew] brought him [Simon] to Jesus. Jesus looked at him and said, "You are Simon son of John. You will be called Cephas" (which, when translated, is Peter)' (John1:42).

A change of name at the time of a call by God is not uncommon in the Bible. When he was ninety two years old and the covenant with him was confirmed by God, Abram's name was changed to Abraham, meaning 'father of a multitude of nations'. When Jacob had striven with God in prayer, his name was changed to 'Israel' (God strives). A change in name denotes a new, God-given task and purpose. God's purpose for Simon was that he would be the rock on which he would build the Church. Although there were times when Peter conspicuously failed to live up to his name, his failure and restoration has given hope and encouragement to all Christian leaders since; nor did Jesus withdraw his purpose and vocation when he failed. As Paul wrote: '...God's gifts and his call are irrevocable' (Romans 11:29).

On a visit to eastern Nigeria, I was speaking to our host bishop about names and their significance amongst the Ibo people in the region. He said that the name of a person could tell you a lot about their family, their place in the family, and the circumstances of their birth. In that society, a name is a clue to the person's history and cultural situation. Names were of similar significance in biblical times; they were clues both to the person's origins and history, and to their vocation.

God has a vocation, a calling, especially for you—to serve him in a particular way. At the same time, he may give you a special awareness of his transcendent glory and presence—whether in worship; in revelation; or in the Scriptures, burning into your consciousness and preparing the way for his 'still small voice'. There may be a feeling in your heart of deep inadequacy, and amazement that you should be caught up in the purposes of God in your village, town or further afield in the world. As he calls you personally, God is promising you a future which is bright with meaning, harnessing your gifts and personality to his plans. A calling from God involved real challenges for Simon Peter; it will for you, too. Although this may mean leaving something familiar and digging up a few roots, it will lead to greater dependence upon him. There will be sacrifices, but there is the deepest fulfilment, too, which comes from working in co-operation with God, in the place that he has planned for you. These things can be seen as God calls people today—now, just as much as on the day Jesus sat in Simon's boat and sent him out fishing.......again! If you are still waiting for God to make clear your vocation in life, be ready to hear from him; and test what you feel that calling to be—by prayer; by being open to the Holy Spirit; by talking it out with wise Christians who know you well; by seeking confirmation of the call from him; by ensuring that what you hear is in line with biblical truth. You may be certain that, if you listen to him in such ways, God will make his call clear to you, and it will be his best—for you, and for his kingdom.

*Lord Jesus, open my ears to hear your voice calling me; give me courage to follow you, and to leave behind whatever I should; help me to trust in your promises, and to embrace the exciting purpose you have for my life. Amen.*

# 5

# Salvation:
# The Woman at the Well

## *Jon Soper*

We begin with St. John's account of this meeting:

Now [Jesus] had to go through Samaria. So he came to a town in Samaria called Sychar, near the plot of ground Jacob had given to his son Joseph. Jacob's well was there, and Jesus, tired as he was from the journey, sat down by the well. It was about the sixth hour.

When a Samaritan woman came to draw water, Jesus said to her, "Will you give me a drink?" (His disciples had gone into the town to buy food.)

The Samaritan woman said to him, "You are a Jew and I am a Samaritan woman. How can you ask me for a drink?" (For Jews do not associate with Samaritans.)

Jesus answered her, "If you knew the gift of God and who it is that asks you for a drink, you would have asked him and he would have given you living water."

"Sir," the woman said, "you have nothing to draw with and the well is deep. Where can you get this living water? Are you greater than our father Jacob, who gave us the well and drank from it himself, as did also his sons and his flocks and herds?"

Jesus answered, "Everyone who drinks this water will be thirsty again, but whoever drinks the water I give him will never thirst. Indeed, the water I give him will become in him a spring of water welling up to eternal life."

The woman said to him, "Sir, give me this water so that I won't get thirsty and have to keep coming here to draw water."

He told her, "Go, call your husband and come back."

"I have no husband," she replied.

Jesus said to her, "You are right when you say you have no husband. The fact is, you have had five husbands, and the man you now have is not your husband. What you have just said is quite true."

"Sir," the woman said, "I can see that you are a prophet. Our fathers worshipped on this mountain, but you Jews claim that the place where we must worship is in Jerusalem."

Jesus declared, "Believe me, woman, a time is coming when you will worship the Father neither on this mountain nor in Jerusalem. You Samaritans worship what you do not know; we worship what we do know, for salvation is from the Jews. Yet a time is coming and has now come when the true worshippers will worship the Father in spirit and truth, for they are the kind of worshippers the Father seeks. God is spirit, and his worshippers must worship in spirit and in truth."

The woman said, "I know that Messiah" (called Christ) "is coming. When he comes, he will explain everything to us."

Then Jesus declared, "I who speak to you am he."

Just then his disciples returned and were surprised to find him talking with a woman. But no one asked, "What do you want?" or "Why are you talking with her?"

Then, leaving her water jar, the woman went back to the town and said to the people, "Come, see a man who told me everything I ever did. Could this be the Christ?" They came out of the town and made their way toward him.

*John 4:4–30*

How Jesus loves to change us! How much he wants to bring transformation to people's lives—to those who have nothing and those who seem to have a great deal. He wants to come and transform us utterly: then we can go out in his name and be used in bringing his transformation to others. In the uncertain times in which we live, it is often said that the people who get on in this life are those who are flexible and therefore able to change, because the pace of change is so much more rapid nowadays. Although God himself is unchanging, we find that change is a continuing feature of our walk with him.

In these meetings with Jesus, what so often strikes us is that lives are dramatically transformed when people encounter him. This is manifestly true in the case of the Samaritan woman, whom Jesus met at a well. At first it seems to be a casual meeting. Jesus is tired and hungry. He has been travelling from Judea back to Galilee, and he has to go through Samaria. He needs a drink; his disciples have gone into town, Sychar, to buy some food. The woman comes out. It is the middle of the day; she is fetching her daily water supply. As a result of that 'casual' meeting, two days later many of the inhabitants of the area were proclaiming that Jesus is the Saviour of the world! The meeting has not only transformed the life of one woman, but much of the town—and very quickly, too. This is what Jesus is about: transformation. During this encounter, Jesus, the Son of God, comes close to the woman. Most of the time, she is unaware of who he is and exactly what is going on—the fact that God Almighty has drawn near to her. It takes her a while to focus on that and understand; then, when she does, it makes all the difference in the world to her. As that realisation dawns, an astonishing change takes place in her life—in the midst of her everyday work, as she carries out the mundane task of getting some water to take back home.

It is her usual midday journey, but what is about to occur could not be more unusual. Jesus asks her for a drink. In that way, taking that initiative, Jesus crosses boundaries in a most striking way: those boundaries which existed between men and women, and boundaries between Jews and Samaritans. In those days, Jews and Samaritans hated each other. In the words "Will you give me a drink?" Jesus, the Son of God, at first appears to put himself in this woman's debt. How often Jesus comes to us where we are!

As the conversation continues, Jesus starts to engage her with a discussion about 'living water'. The dialogue takes place at two levels. She is talking about drinking water; he is talking about the living water which is a picture of the power of God—or the Holy Spirit. As they talk, she responds in several ways. First of all, she is very surprised—by the very fact that Jesus asks her for a drink. She says, "You are a Jew and I am a Samaritan woman. How can you ask me for a drink?" As he continues, talking about the living water, she seems to become rather sarcastic with him, saying: "...you have nothing to draw with and the well is deep. Where can you get this living water? Are you greater than our father Jacob, who gave us the well...?" Yet Jesus persists and she is intrigued— soon she is saying, "Sir, give me this water so that I won't get thirsty and have to keep coming here to draw water." She still has not quite got it, because she thinks that if she has the living water she will not need to drink physical water any more, so avoiding the labour of her daily journey.

We see how Jesus leads the woman to think more deeply. If you drink water, you are soon thirsty again. Jesus steps into her unsatisfying everyday life and gives her something extraordinary, permanent and deeply satisfying. We are shown an ordinary life being broken into by something absolutely wonderful. This may be your experience of God as well, especially when you became a Christian. You may have been just going along in your day to day existence, and suddenly realised that God has drawn close to you. Jesus wants to transform our everyday lives—not just when we come to church or go to home group or Alpha, or during our own prayers in the morning or evening, but also as we are just pottering around, doing whatever we do. We may be at work or making a cup of tea; in any situation at all we may suddenly be aware that God is very close to us. We may have an experience of suddenly realising he is telling us something or calling us to something; or maybe summoning us to a life-changing decision to believe and trust in Jesus, and so become alive in him.

Jesus also transformed the messy life of the woman at the well. She had had five husbands and was now living with another man. She could obviously attract men, but found it difficult to keep them. Unable to get into a long term, committed, intimate relationship, she was addicted to 'serial monogamy'. Her lifestyle would have been thought extremely immoral. Her relationships seem to have been emotionally unsatisfying and were very unsatisfactory. Jesus put it very kindly when he asks her to call her husband. Then she has to admit that she has no husband. When Jesus tells her that he knows she has had five husbands and is now living with someone else, he shows that he knows her completely. Then she is able to go away and say to the people of her town, "Come, see a man who told me everything I ever did." She has suddenly found someone completely different from anyone she has ever known before; she has experienced a meeting from which she will begin to find a hitherto elusive emotional satisfaction and many other blessings. We do not know how her life ends up. But we suspect, from the account, that she is so changed that her life starts to get sorted out. She left everything to follow Jesus. She came with her water jar, to fetch water, and now she has left it there to go and tell others. Isn't that amazing? In the same way, the disciples left everything to follow him.

The woman's life changes spiritually. At first, she brings her spiritual life into the conversation as a bit of a red herring. When Jesus spoke those accurate words about her five husbands, she answered most perceptively: "Sir... I can see that you are a prophet." Then she began going on about "Our fathers worshipped on this mountain...." and gets into a conversation about worship. It is a diversion from the personal exposure of her life, but Jesus dignifies her by continuing with it: talking theology with her, which is something a Jewish rabbi would simply not have done with a woman. He talks about worship with her because she has brought up the subject. But her worship, and her appreciation of God, as a Samaritan of that time, were very partial. Her people knew the first five books of the Bible and had an impersonal view of God who was worshipped on Mount Gerizim, where they were located.

It may be that before becoming a Christian you, too, had an 'impersonal' concept of God. Recently a woman said to me, "I really like this whole business about God; well I quite like it, anyway, but I have big problems with Jesus." It is a very common attitude which poses a big problem, because Jesus is the main man: he is what it is all about! In the matter of faith, everything revolves around Jesus. He himself made this abundantly clear, as he talked about worship, saying, "a time is coming and has now come when the true worshippers will worship the Father in spirit and truth...." And who is the truth? Jesus is the truth. He says, later on in St. John's Gospel, "I am the...truth...." It is extremely personal. It is not just abstract doctrine. We come to Jesus, worshipping him personally, closely and intimately, so that we can really know him.

So Jesus is taking the woman from the abstract to the very personal. She tries one last delaying tactic, saying that she knows Messiah, who would explain everything, is coming. Jesus does not accept any more delay, but replies, "I who speak to you am he." This is one of the clearest statements of divine identity—made, extraordinarily, to someone to whom the disciples would never have expected Jesus to speak! Here is the 'crunch opportunity', as Jesus comes amazingly close, showing her who he really is. He makes available this 'living water'; he can bring true fulfilment to her life, giving her a real, personal spiritual life. He utters those words and that is when she leaves her water jar, shooting back to town to say: "Come, see a man who told me everything I ever did...."

Amazing changes take place in the woman's life. John depicts her as a model disciple. She leaves everything to follow Jesus; she then has a testimony to give to others, including her own people— and she does so, boldly and effectively. The account concludes with the result of her witness. When her own people hear her speak about Jesus, many become believers. They urge Jesus to stay, and because of his words to them which they can hear for themselves, many more of them believe in him. They are able to say, "We no longer believe just because of what you said; now we have heard for ourselves, and we know that this man really is the Saviour of the world." (See John 4:39–42). What a remarkable series of changes had resulted from an apparently casual meeting at the well, as many lives now began to be transformed.

God brings special opportunities to us, too. You may be able to recall moments when you have known his closeness: when he has revealed something of himself to you and extraordinary change has resulted, or perhaps there has been a calling to something new in your life. Be alert to God's presence—ready to meet with Jesus. It took the woman at the well a while to work out what was happening; it may have taken the rest of her life to discover all the implications of her meeting with him. We need to wait on God, ready for moments when his love is being clearly revealed, when he shows us more of himself or speaks to us in a particular way. Such attentiveness demands patience and perseverance. It can be costly. Think of something you really want and value, then ask yourself whether it is *worth* waiting for; recall that what you await from God is the most precious and wonderful thing you can possibly have—a closer, deeper walk with Jesus. God wants us to be ready for him each day, so that we are ready to respond positively to anything he gives us. The initiative is his; as we become ready in our hearts and minds, he is able to bring about transformation. If you have never met Jesus, begin to look attentively for him. If you sense that he has already come close, but you are not quite sure whether this is real, I encourage you to respond with a simple step: simply begin to talk to him; and talk with some Christian friends. Soon you will find that there is something real going on, and discover for yourself; as that woman at the well did; as her Samaritan community did; and as countless millions of others have done down the centuries—that he is indeed the Way, the Truth and the Life.

*Heavenly Father, thank you so much that you want us all to be changed, to be more like Jesus. I do want that for myself; I want to know you more closely. I ask you to help me at each moment to be alert, waiting on you; aware of your presence and your love for me. Amen.*

# 6

# Compassion:
# The Widow of Nain

*Nigel Rawlinson*

Compassion is a hallmark of the love of God, and is shown profoundly in the ministry of Jesus. Defined as 'a sense of pity inclining one to help or be merciful', it is a feeling that leads to action and involvement. There is also a sense of restoration or healing.

The account of the meeting with Jesus of the widow of Nain shows us the compassion of God. Luke the physician often emphasised this feature of Jesus' ministry. Reflect on the account in his Gospel of how Jesus wept over Jerusalem, saying, "If you, even you, had only known on this day what would bring you peace—but now it is hidden from your eyes" (Luke 19:42). Only Luke records the depth of Jesus' struggle and anguish at Gethsemane (Luke 22:39–44). Jesus knew his task: what he had to do to save a people loved by God his Father. In the garden there is perfect abandonment, at a huge cost. We watch him in prayer, his sweat like drops of blood, with the weight of the day ahead. He knew there was no other way, and he shows ultimate compassion.

His encounter with a bereaved widow is intimate and personal, depicted as though it were a chance meeting. Although this incident happened two thousand years ago, it is vivid because it describes an experience that we will all have felt at some time. As we think of the scene, we can feel the sadness of the widow. Jesus ministers to her; we can feel that, too. This story brings the reality of God's compassion right into our hearts today. Why is this important? To answer this, we need to ask ourselves a question: are we really compassionate, both with ourselves and others? We are living in a culture which undermines true compassion. We tend to be self-critical, defining ourselves by our failings. With others, we all too often look for reward or repayment. Our 'compassion' can become rationed and conditional. The more we reflect on this in the light of God's revealed nature, the more we see the depth of his love for us—just as we are. Then we are challenged to show this love to others.

We are not perfect—we know that. Through Jesus we can be forgiven—we believe that. But how often we let ourselves get demoralised! Do you set spiritual targets for your behaviour or discipline that you cannot reach, perhaps setting the goal of reading several Christian books, or giving up some things, only to discover, again and again, that you go on failing? Then, sometimes, the mistake is made of feeling that you cannot ask God's forgiveness so often for the same thing, so you settle for things as they are, feeling demoralised and spoiled — and instead set yet more targets. Such an attitude is itself sinful. We come to believe that there is a limit to God's forgiveness. Doubts creep in. Can we really be freed from this guilt? We fail to see the way out of the mire, becoming stuck in the role of 'miserable sinner'. Then we become vulnerable. This is a rich opportunity for spiritual attack—Satan loves knocking a Christian's confidence in Jesus; we fail to have compassion upon ourselves.

If this is how we are like with ourselves, what about our attitude towards others? We are comfortable with those who are like us, with whom we get on and 'speak the same language'. We may like *them*, but what about the stranger? There are so many examples that challenge us. Could impatience ever lead to road rage if you find yourself following an old person driving at 29 mph in a 40 mph zone? You may think not, but what if we include verbal comment and use of the car horn? Or how about the Christian who worships in a different way and doesn't like *our* songs. Do we enjoy sharing together in the love of God, or do we write them off as being spiritually weak? How often have we said (or thought): "There's no way I can help him. Why should I? He can sort himself out!" A different problem is 'compassion exhaustion'. We see so much suffering in the news that we become immune to it.

So, both personally in our own lives, and outwardly in our

relationships with others, our compassion falls short. Often these two go together. The more uncomfortable we are with ourselves, the less tolerant we are of others. Contrast this with God's infinite compassion for each of us. The more we become aware of our need for it, the more we can understand the nature of God's compassion. When we understand his compassion for us, we can then have compassion for ourselves, and also, therefore, have compassion for others. That is deeply healing. So let us read this story from Luke's Gospel, placing ourselves there. Could we be the recipients of this love? Could we seek it?

Soon afterward, Jesus went to a town called Nain, and his disciples and a large crowd went along with him. As he approached the town gate, a dead person was being carried out—the only son of his mother, and she was a widow. And a large crowd from the town was with her. When the Lord saw her, his heart went out to her and he said, "Don't cry."

Then he went up and touched the coffin, and those carrying it stood still. He said, "Young man, I say to you, get up!"

The dead man sat up and began to talk, and Jesus gave him back to his mother. They were all filled with awe and praised God. "A great prophet has appeared among us," they said. "God has come to help his people." This news about Jesus spread throughout Judea and the surrounding country.

*Luke 7:11–17*

Jesus is travelling from Lake Galilee to Nain, a border town some twenty five miles southwest of Capernaum. He is with his disciples. Imagine the scene. This is a very sad and vivid picture. Jesus meets the procession. Here is the dead son, the only son, of a widow. In Jewish society she was doomed, lost, having no one to care for her. We know nothing more about her or her family. It is most likely that she was just an ordinary person—like us. Sense the mood; hear the wailing; see the dust; be bustled by the large crowd; then glimpse the woman in the middle, supported by her friends. She must have felt desperately lost. We read that Jesus intervened, and that his heart went out to her and he said, "don't cry". The first thing we notice is that this was one way communication. There is no indication here that she knew him or sought him, and we are reminded that true compassion does not insist upon response—it is not conditional. Look again at the sequence of events: Jesus sees her; his heart goes out, and then he says, "don't cry". The directive "don't cry" sets up a feeling of anticipation: something is about to happen. Here is a reaction, leading to action: a feeling with consequences. Compassion results in something happening. Jesus is now clearly centre stage. All eyes must have been on him. Ignoring the ritual regulations concerning the 'uncleanness' of the dead body, he touches the coffin and the procession stops. He brings the son back to life and gives him back to his mother. Note that it is the woman who is the main beneficiary of this story. It was the sight of her that prompted the involvement of Jesus. It is her future that is made more secure by the return of her only son. We are not told anything about his reaction, though we can imagine it. We learn that, "...The people were filled with awe and praised God..." and that they acknowledged the truth that: "God has come to help his people." Yes, he did so then, and he still does now.

Let us affirm for ourselves that realisation which dawned on those people. It is as relevant today as ever, yet, in our age, so many people hear about Jesus and laugh, ridicule—or simply reject. They say, "this is not for me".

Be encouraged! Although you might sometimes feel very distant from our Lord, you are not alone in that experience. Perhaps the cause seems to be a recurring weakness, or a memory that comes back—something you thought you had sorted out. You may feel trapped in that distant place: unsure, even scared of being separated from him. This happened to me. Things rapidly went out of perspective. The 'distance' was of my own making. I felt I could not ask for help again. What foolish arrogance! Could I limit the love of God? I could not work it out. The resolution of my problem was given to me through a stranger one evening. Once again, I was shown the depth of God's love and compassion as the person asked me to read these words in a service, and I realised they were meant for me:

Spiritual life is life drawn from the Holy Spirit, who raised Jesus from the dead.... The Spirit within you will bear fruit of simplicity and goodness, modesty and joy, sobriety and gentleness. He will give you interior freedom and bring your love to perfection. He will make you into a new person.

So don't carry on a futile battle against yourself, don't divide yourself into good and evil, resist the temptation to analyse yourself. Turn your attention to the Lord instead, and be deeply receptive. Accept yourself in his light and concentrate on the mission you have to accomplish.

God's Spirit will bring you to simplicity in an undivided dedication to Him and to your fellow creatures. He gives you no programme

COMPASSION

but the chance to turn yourself to love hour by hour. And so spiritual life is not a burden but a liberating vocation. It is much more a matter of simplifying than of complicated methods and extraordinary performances.

*Rule for a new brother* © *1973, 1986*
*Darton Longman and Todd (Used by permission)*

God was calling me back. Through this stranger, he showed me the way home. I saw again the infinite nature of God's compassion. I was able to feel loved, accepted and forgiven. That gave me a new peace in myself—the peace of God. So, at times when you feel distant, be gentle with yourself. Refocus on God. He always loves; and he forgives all who come to him in penitence, trusting in the sacrifice of Jesus. Know that you are *totally* loved by God. The spiritual life will emerge. In the service of Holy Communion, the wonderful compassion of God is clearly seen. We come together in the presence of God, eat and drink, and as we hear and see the act of thanksgiving we can hear Jesus assuring us that we are accepted and forgiven in him. Then we must remember our commission to others. When we know this compassion of God in ourselves, it is so good that we have to tell others. This is best done by showing others the same compassion that we have received from the Lord. When we do this, we become an instrument for God to reach out—even when we are not aware that this is what is happening.

I heard of a patient in hospital, recently diagnosed as having a terminal disease. He asked to see a chaplain, to whom he spoke of being deeply troubled by an event which had taken place during the Second World War. He and his brother were in action in the Far East. His brother was killed; he had been unable to save him. Things were left unsaid and unfinished. Now, more than half a century later, he was asking for God's forgiveness, and was distressed because he could not possibly see how it could happen. The chaplain was able to say: "Yes, you are loved, accepted, and forgiven."

This is God's unconditional compassion, and it is often up to us to tell others about it. We are called to show compassion to all people. This is 'one way' ministry, like Jesus' compassion upon the widow. God is then working through us. Of course, 'all people' includes not only those outside church, but those within our church, too! People who do not yet believe must look with some amazement at the lack of compassion amongst Christian

53

communities. There is so much intolerance: it is disgraceful, and does the spread of the Gospel much harm. To show compassion is, by contrast, one of the best ways to show God's love—it is God's love shining through us, and so is a powerful means of mission.

Finally, a word of warning: we are not to be aloof in this process. We give our hearts, just as Jesus did. We become involved. We are vulnerable to hurt as we minister the love of God to others and become aware of their pains and burdens. We cannot do this on our own. Just as it was in Gethsemane, when an angel strengthened Jesus, so God strengthens us. Take care to rest in the Lord. Prayer is vital. We cannot hold all these burdens. We would 'blow up'! We must hand them to God. He will keep us involved, if he needs us. This is *his* work.

The people said, "God has come to help his people." Yes, God has come to help us. So be compassionate with yourself, and in so doing realise God's compassion for you. It is offered all the time; it is there in Jesus, for us to receive from him. May the peace of God rule your hearts, as you remember that the Lord helps us to show compassion. As we minister, Jesus takes the pain, and his healing love is brought to the person in distress.

*Lord Jesus, teach us the depth of your compassion—for ourselves, and for all those we meet. Amen.*

# 7

# Disputation:
# The Man Born Blind

## *Patrick Whitworth*

---

You might be surprised to learn that the longest recorded meeting
between anyone and Jesus in the Gospels is this one. John, who is
the only evangelist to record this meeting, devotes an entire
chapter to the encounter and its spiritual implications. It contains
one of the most bitter exchanges between Jesus and the Pharisees,
but it has at its centre one of the most feisty and memorable
individuals in the whole of the New Testament. He has the most
marvellous wit, combined with complete disdain for the humbug
of the Pharisees. It has the three vital ingredients of a great
Johannine encounter: a highly significant saying of Jesus, a sign
or miracle which served to illustrate the meaning of the saying,
and a fierce dispute with the Jewish leaders.

As he went along, he [Jesus] saw a man blind from birth. His disciples
asked him, "Rabbi, who sinned, this man or his parents, that he was
born blind?"

"Neither this man nor his parents sinned," said Jesus, "but this
happened so that the work of God might be displayed in his life. As
long as it is day, we must do the work of him who sent me. Night is
coming, when no one can work. While I am in the world, I am the
light of the world." Having said this, he spat on the ground, made
some mud with the saliva, and put it on the man's eyes. "Go," he
told him, "wash in the Pool of Siloam" (this word means Sent). So
the man went and washed, and came home seeing.

His neighbours and those who had formerly seen him begging

asked, "Isn't this the same man who used to sit and beg?" Some claimed that he was.

Others said, "No, he only looks like him."

But he himself insisted, "I am the man."

"How then were your eyes opened?" they demanded.

He replied, "The man they call Jesus made some mud and put it on my eyes. He told me to go to Siloam and wash. So I went and washed, and then I could see."

"Where is this man?" they asked him.

"I don't know," he said.

They brought to the Pharisees the man who had been blind. Now the day on which Jesus had made the mud and opened the man's eyes was a Sabbath. Therefore the Pharisees also asked him how he had received his sight. "He put mud on my eyes," the man replied, "and I washed, and now I see."

Some of the Pharisees said, "This man is not from God, for he does not keep the Sabbath."

But others asked, "How can a sinner do such miraculous signs?" So they were divided.

Finally they turned again to the blind man, "What have you to say about him? It was your eyes he opened."

The man replied, "He is a prophet."

The Jews still did not believe that he had been blind and had received his sight until they sent for the man's parents.

"Is this your son?" they asked. "Is this the one you say was born blind? How is it that now he can see?"

"We know he is our son," the parents answered, "and we know he was born blind. But how he can see now, or who opened his eyes, we don't know. Ask him. He is of age; he will speak for himself." His parents said this because they were afraid of the Jews, for already the Jews had decided that anyone who acknowledged that Jesus was the Christ would be put out of the synagogue. That was why his parents said, "He is of age; ask him."

A second time they summoned the man who had been blind. "Give glory to God!" they said. "We know this man is a sinner."

He replied, "Whether he is a sinner or not, I don't know. One thing I do know. I was blind but now I see!"

Then they asked him, "What did he do to you? How did he open your eyes?"

He answered, "I have told you already, and you did not listen. Why do you want to hear it again? Do you want to become his disciples, too?"

Then they hurled insults at him and said, "You are this fellow's disciple! We are disciples of Moses! We know that God spoke to Moses, but as for this fellow, we don't even know where he comes from."

# DISPUTATION

The man answered, "Now that is remarkable! You don't know where he comes from, yet he opened my eyes! We know that God does not listen to sinners. He listens to the godly man who does his will. Nobody has ever heard of opening the eyes of a man born blind. If this man were not from God, he could do nothing."

To this they replied, "You were steeped in sin at birth; how dare you lecture us!" And they threw him out.

Jesus heard that they had thrown him out, and when he found him, he said, "Do you believe in the Son of Man?"

"Who is he, sir?" the man asked. "Tell me so that I may believe in him."

Jesus said, "You have now seen him; in fact, he is the one speaking with you."

Then the man said, "Lord, I believe," and he worshipped him.

Jesus said, "For judgment I have come into this world, so that the blind will see and those who see will become blind."

Some Pharisees who were with him heard him say this and asked, "What? Are we blind too?"

Jesus said, "If you were blind, you would not be guilty of sin; but now that you claim you can see, your guilt remains."

*John 9:1–41*

The key to understanding the significance of this meeting lies in one of Jesus' concluding remarks. In fact, frequently Jesus summarises his teaching or his parables or actions with a pithy concluding remark or comment which is the key to unlocking the meaning of the teaching or action. The significant remark here is, "For judgment I have come into the world, so that the blind will see and those who see will become blind." As so often with the sayings of Jesus, a complete reversal is described, as in the saying "The first shall be last and the last shall be first." Here, those who were blind find themselves seeing, and those who thought they could see find they are blind. As usual, the kingdom of God is 'topsy turvy' and the King delights in turning things on their head! In this case, the outcome is related to the dual effect of light.

This chapter and meeting is centred on the theme of light, and the great 'I am' saying of Jesus: "I am the light of the world." We know that the Gospel of John is built around these 'I am' sayings and the 'signs' that accompany them. Here, the saying and the sign have the principal purpose of being a further witness to Jesus and who he is; indeed Jesus goes as far as to say that the cause of the man's blindness was that, "the work of God might be displayed in his life" (v.3). The dual effect of light, both physically and spiritually, is either to attract and illuminate, or to repel and blind.

Just as this is true in the natural world so is it true in the spiritual realm as well. Generally speaking, light attracts, whether it is moths to a house light on a summer's evening, or a boat to shore lights when seeking landfall. But there are occasions when light can damage, or even blind, as when earthquake victims who have been rescued from some subterranean ordeal are brought to the surface, having spent days in darkness. Response to light depends either on what your eyes have grown accustomed to or whether light or darkness is beneficial to a person's or animal's existence. In the natural world, some animals, like bats or badgers, thrive under the cover of darkness, whilst others are only active in the light.

Equally, spiritually, people may either be drawn to the Light of the world or may be repelled by him. At the outset of his Gospel, John warns us of the divisive effect of the coming of the Light of the world. Earlier in the Gospel, Jesus had analysed why some would come to the Light and others would not: "This is the verdict: Light has come into the world, but men loved darkness instead of light because their deeds were evil. Everyone who does evil hates the light, and will not come into the light for fear that his deeds will be exposed. But whoever lives by the truth comes into the light, so that it may be seen plainly that what he has done has been done through God" (John 3:19–21).

Now, in a single incident and encounter, all these spiritual principles about light and darkness are focused in a meeting between Jesus and the man born blind, with its repercussions for the Pharisees. There are three categories of people caught up in this dramatic miracle and ensuing bitter controversy: the man, his relatives and neighbours, and the Pharisees. Let us begin with the man himself.

Because of his disability, he had become a beggar. As far as the disciples were concerned, he was initially a theological exhibit in a seminar taking place between them and Jesus. "Rabbi," they asked, "who sinned, this man or his parents, that he was born blind?" They were, in this question, the forbears to that school of theology which holds that physical disability is invariably linked to moral failure. This outlook was also generally held amongst Jesus' contemporaries, and is still prevalent in some religious systems. However, Jesus is emphatic that no link could be made in this man's case between his blindness and supposed moral failure on his own part or that of his parents. Jesus replied that, "neither this man nor his parents sinned". In fact, Jesus indicated that, in this man's case, his very blindness was so that the glory of God might be shown.

However, a seminar with Jesus was always dynamic, never purely academic. It was charged with both urgency and power. Action was urgent because, "night is coming, when no one can work", so "as long as it is day, we must do the work of him who sent me." With this imperative in mind, Jesus prepared to heal him. He then did something unusual, even by his standards! Jesus 'spat on the ground, made some mud with the saliva, and put it on the man's eyes', then told him to, "Go, wash in the Pool of Siloam." On two other occasions in the Gospels, Jesus uses spit or saliva in healing miracles, ministering to those who were blind. I have yet to hear of churches where the prayer for healing includes a good dose of saliva, and no doubt if there was one it would fall foul of health and safety regulations at best, and at worst it would be laughed out of town. But why did Jesus set about healing this man this way, when presumably a word would have sufficed? There are a number of explanations. The most plausible is that by using 'things' in the cure—saliva, dust and the water in the Pool of Siloam— Jesus provoked the man to an act of faith in his word. These things did not effect the cure: the cure was through the power of Christ; but, by using them, Jesus gave the man both an opportunity to obey his word and a memorable event, which would help him when it came to his interrogation later on, both by his neighbours and the Pharisees. The making of the clay by Jesus would also have provoked the dispute with the Pharisees, who regarded it as work and so a contravention of the rules governing the Sabbath. Another allegorical explanation for the use of dust and saliva in the cure was that just as man was formed by the Word and dust in Genesis chapter two, so, here, a man's blindness is repaired by the same combination of Word and dust. One girl, on being told by her devout mother that humans had been created out of dust and would return to such, was once observed looking long and hard under her bed. Asked what she was doing she said she was looking at a lot of people coming and going!

If our hero in this story thought that his miraculous healing was the beginning of a carefree life, he was gloriously mistaken! No sooner had he reached home than there was, firstly, a controversy over his identity! Some said he was the self same man, others that he only looked liked him and that he was really someone different! It reads like a veritable pantomime, but it serves to show that so striking was the change that Jesus brought to this man's life that he was virtually unrecognisable. In order to get to the bottom of what was going on, the religious sleuth hounds were called for. They would investigate what had happened and find out who this man really was. The trial begins!

The court is assembled and the chief witness is brought in. At the outset, the proceedings seem fairly measured. The testimony of the man sounds faintly ridiculous, "He put mud on my eyes, and I washed, and now I see," yet the reality of a man once blind but now seeing stares them in the face! If they believe his story, then they face a deeper question: "who is this Jesus?" There are various bits of evidence to consider: the identity of the man, his extraordinary story; the fact that the cure involved 'work' and took place on the Sabbath; and the claim that a remarkable miracle had taken place.

At the first hearing (vv. 13–23), the Pharisees heard the man's story. With his parents' help, they established the man's identity as the beggar who had been born blind, took on board that the miracle had happened on the Sabbath, and were beginning to consider the identity of Jesus. It appeared that some were beginning to open up the issue of the identity of Jesus, some branded Jesus a sinner as he had performed this miracle on the Sabbath, whilst others asked, "How can a sinner do such miraculous signs?" But behind this seemingly even-handed treatment of the evidence, there now looms a statement which shows that their conclusions will, in the end, be based on grounds that have nothing to do with evidence. For John tells us that the man's parents were intimidated by the fact that, "the Jews had decided that anyone who acknowledged that Jesus was the Christ would be put out of the synagogue." Since, therefore, there was only one conclusion that the investigation could come to, the evidence was of no avail.

All too frequently, this dynamic applies to people's conclusions about who Jesus is. The evidence that he is God's Son, able to heal, restore and forgive, is strong but it is buried with an underlying fear that yielding control of your life to him will diminish rather than enhance your life. The Pharisees were not so much frightened as determined to keep control of their power over the people and their own agenda, so they became 'blind' to all evidence that Jesus might be the Christ.

The second hearing of this investigation showed both their own increasing blindness and the greater illumination of the man who had been blind. It is after this section that Jesus speaks of his role in judgment, and the reversal of the expected order of things, the blind seeing, and 'those who see' becoming blind. (See v.39). This part of the examination has an entirely different feel to it. It begins with a rather peremptory instruction to the formerly blind man: "Give glory to God!"; far from meaning what it literally says, which incidentally the man had been doing, it was code for 'do what we say' or 'jolly well agree with us'. Then they gave their conclusion about Jesus: "We know this man is a sinner." It is now that the man shows his grit, courage and impeccable logic. His now classic answer ("Whether he is a sinner or not, I don't know. One thing I do know. I was blind but now I see!") is famous for its assertion of empirical fact over vain theological speculation. As far as the man was concerned, it was hopeless to hold to prejudice in the face of the one fact which was undeniable to him, which was that once he was blind and now he could see. More than standing his ground, he becomes impatient with their obtuseness, taunting them on their request to hear the story of his healing again, with the gibe, "Do you want to become his disciples, too?" At this point, the hearing degenerates into farce; a discernible downward spiral takes place, where hostility turns to abuse and, for a while, looks like becoming violent. Of course, this is precisely what does happen in the later trial of Jesus, which this foreshadows. However, still the man gives as good as he gets when the Pharisees say of Jesus that they do not even know where he comes from. With enraged sarcasm, he replies: "Now that is remarkable! You don't know where he comes from, yet he opened my eyes. We know that God does not listen to sinners. He listens to the godly man who does his will. Nobody has ever heard of opening the eyes of a man born blind. If this man were not from God, he could do nothing."

Here was theology! Here was a beggar turned Regius Professor! They could not bear it. Resorting both to violence and verbal abuse, they went back to the starting point, about which Jesus had had to correct the disciples, both telling him that he was steeped in sin at birth, and expelling him.

The epilogue to this 'courtroom drama' follows. Jesus hears what has happened and finds the man. His intention is to add spiritual sight to the physical sight that has been restored, and to which the man has so boldly testified. In a moment of rare intimacy, which makes this story so compelling and reminiscent of the meeting with the woman at the well, Jesus tells the enquiring man that he is the Son of Man. Like Thomas, at the end of the Gospel, the man says, "Lord, I believe", and proceeds to worship him.

So we return to the central didactic point of this encounter— between Jesus and the man; the man and the Pharisees; and between the Pharisees and Jesus. The presence of Jesus brings judgment, in the same way as light brings with it a reaction. Either it is welcomed and enjoyed, or else, because our eyes have become accustomed to darkness, we prefer that darkness to the light. The Pharisees refused to come to the light, because they did not wish to lose control of their power. The man longed for sight, and was prepared both to believe and obey Jesus. His family and friends realised what had happened to their relative and friend but, as yet, were intimidated by the Pharisees. As Jesus demonstrated, the blind could now see; and those who prided themselves on a sight which left them in the centre of their world were blind; worse than that, because they claimed they could see, they were guilty too! As for us listeners to this story, it is our responsibility to come to the Light and pray that our blindness be taken away, so that we can clearly see **the way**. We are all blind, until the light in the face of Jesus Christ has shone into our hearts. The worst thing any of us can do is to call our blindness sight. The best thing any of us can do is pray that God would shine his light into our hearts.

*Lord God, thank you for showing us that Jesus has the power to bring both spiritual and physical sight; fill our hearts with the light of Jesus, the true Light. Amen.*

# 8

# Inclusion:
# The Syro-Phoenician Woman

## Patrick Whitworth

Exclusion has become a political word. The government has set up 'exclusion units' to deal with the problem of people, especially in our cities, who, through whatever reason, find themselves on the outside of society. The causes of their exclusion are complex: usually a mixture of economic, psychological, spiritual and domestic factors. It is the interplay of these causes which makes the treatment of the problem of 'exclusion' so hard—and no doubt those responsible for the government initiatives are finding this to be the case. The problem existed in Jesus' day. Categories of people found themselves systematically excluded from Jewish society and, frequently, Jesus found himself dealing with them. In fact, the tightly drawn regulations that guarded first century Jewish society created a large number of 'untouchables'. These included lepers, those with skin diseases, notorious sinners—such as tax-collectors working for the occupying power—prostitutes, the demonised, and the largest category of all: the Gentiles. Paul speaks about a dividing wall of hostility between Jew and Gentile, and it was this wall, and the exclusion which resulted from it, that Jesus had come to blast away. In this meeting, as with a number of others, Jesus encounters a woman in great need, who found herself excluded from the promises of Israel. We take up the record of the encounter from Mark:

> Jesus left that place and went to the vicinity of Tyre. He entered a

house and did not want anyone to know it; yet he could not keep his presence secret. In fact, as soon as she heard about him, a woman whose little daughter was possessed by an evil spirit came and fell at his feet. The woman was a Greek, born in Syrian Phoenicia. She begged Jesus to drive the demon out of her daughter.

"First let the children eat all they want," he told her, "for it is not right to take the children's bread and toss it to their dogs."

"Yes, Lord," she replied, "but even the dogs under the table eat the children's crumbs."

Then he told her, "For such a reply you may go; the demon has left your daughter."

She went home and found her child lying on the bed, and the demon gone.

*Mark 7:24–30*

This meeting moved through a number of stages: a retreat which was disturbed; a 'riddle' posed; a riposte of faith and release from harm. We shall look at each in turn.

Jesus, as quite often happened in his ministry, was trying to get some 'space', some peace and quiet, as we would say. However, as equally frequently happened, he found that this was hard to find, because of his 'fame'. In this case, Jesus had made considerable effort to find a retreat, and had gone outside Israel's borders to Tyre, in present day Lebanon.

You can imagine the frame of mind with which the average clergyman or minister would approach the prospect of a seaside retreat, away for a few days from his or her responsibilities. He would be looking forward to a few days away from the delightful but demanding parishioners, from the incessant telephone calls and emails!

In fact Jesus had been involved in controversy with the Pharisees. In the verses preceding this meeting, Mark tells us that Jesus had had a stormy discussion with them, when they had accused him with the question: 'Why don't your disciples live according to the tradition of the elders instead of eating their food with 'unclean' hands?' (See Mark 7:5.)

This question had led on to some hard-hitting teaching by Jesus, both about the emptiness of some of their traditions, because through them they subverted God's commands, and about the superficiality of their ablutions before meals, because they failed to seek cleansing for their grubby hearts. At the end of this encounter, Jesus might well have needed a little space; hence, Mark tells us at the beginning of the meeting which we are considering here, that, 'Jesus left that place [where, presumably, he had had this argument with the Pharisees] and went to the vicinity of Tyre.' We may think of him as having arrived in or near Tyre, at the 'holiday cottage' which he had been lent. In fact, the retreat was to be shortlived.

Just as royals and 'stars' are followed by the intrusive paparazzi, with their huge camera lenses, so Jesus was soon sought out by people with deep needs that only he could meet! There was a knock at the door, and a desperate woman threw herself at his feet; he knew that his presence there was no secret. The retreat had ended before it had begun! His cover was blown. The safe house was discovered, and there was a new demand to be met from his inexhaustible supply of power driven by compassion. However, the moment she opened her mouth, or maybe when he set eyes on her, Jesus knew that she was not a Jew, but a Greek of the region of Syrian Phoenicia. Having stated her desperate need, which was that her daughter be released from demonic possession, Jesus replied with a statement that was more akin to a riddle.

Imagine going to your doctor with a severe problem and he made your treatment conditional on solving a riddle rather than filling in a form! You would be surprised! It appears that Jesus gave this woman a riddle to solve, which would ultimately be a test of both her faith and her understanding. On hearing her request, Jesus said to her: "First let the children eat all they want, for it is not right to take the children's bread and toss it to their dogs." This reply appears neither to be encouraging nor complimentary to the woman, for the word 'children' refers to the Israelites and the word 'dogs' seems to be a colloquial expression for the Gentiles. So a paraphrase of Jesus' reply might be, 'wait your turn; you are not invited to the party—at least not yet!'

But Jesus' reply was intended as a test for the woman: a test of her faith and understanding, rather than a closing of the door in her face. In fact, the door was left ajar for her to push open—which she did, with gusto. The small but significant opening Jesus left for her was the word 'first' —a little word we come across in an encounter between Jesus and another woman (see Chapter 11 *Deception*). What this word meant was that there was an economy in God's activity, an order of priority to his working: the Messiah was sent to the children of Israel *first*, but it was simply a question of time before the Gentiles (and this woman was one) would be included in the promises of grace, in the New Covenant. Seeing that Jesus had left the door ajar for her, she pushed through with a reply which was full of spirit and wit. It was a reply that had a character often present in the reactions of 'outsiders' to him, and it was the sort of answer Jesus loved to hear.

Before moving on to the essence of the woman's reply, it is worth reflecting on Jesus' challenge to this woman: Jesus does not give us what we want without making us think carefully about what we are asking for; or, sometimes, refining our faith by making us wait before his reply is given or action occurs. Often, this pause for thought, or refining of our faith, serves to show both God and ourselves how much we want something. Clearly, the woman here was driven by the natural and powerful desire to see her daughter made better. She was not going to relinquish easily her hope of healing and deliverance for her daughter. Nor should we give up on some vision or plan that we believe is of God, when it does not quickly fall into our lap.

I remember, early on in my Christian life, a young couple believing that they had been called to work in Burundi; they had been accepted by a missionary society to work there, but no visas were forthcoming to enable them to enter the country. Nonetheless, they waited expectantly, and told the church they would be going! The visas did, indeed, arrive—the day before their journey! Whatever Jesus was looking for in this woman, he clearly found. It is time to look more closely at her reply: 'Yes, Lord, but even the dogs under the table eat the children's crumbs.'

Apparently, the Greek word for dog here means 'pet dog', so softening the possible 'rudeness'; Jesus seems not to be referring to her as some stray, uncared-for animal! In any event, the woman does not appear to have been put off by the response of Jesus. As we may so often reflect about dialogue in the Gospels, *although we have the words of Jesus, we have neither the inflection of his voice nor the accompanying look and body language*. Although the words may appear to us a little bleak, it is quite probable that they were said as a challenge, inviting that spirited reply; and maybe the look in Jesus' eye invited her to come back at him.

Whether or not this was the case, that is certainly what she did. In fact, she replied in kind. Taking up his illustration of pet dogs, she rejoined that even dogs at home enjoy the benefits of crumbs from the family table. We have a dog, and his favourite position at meal times is under the kitchen table; some things have not changed in two thousand years! The woman's reply showed great understanding and remarkable faith.

Firstly, she understood that Jesus was a Jew, and primarily concerned with ministering to the Jewish people. Whether, like the woman at the well, she understood that he was the Messiah, we cannot be sure; but she did understand that the 'meal' Jesus had come to bring was intended initially for the Jewish people. Nevertheless, she also picked up from Jesus' remark that the banquet he had come to bring was not confined to the Jews. After all, Jesus had said that 'first' the meal would be served to the Jews. He did not say that the Gentiles would be excluded for all time. So, with impeccable understanding, she pressed her claim by saying that even the pet dogs of the house benefited from the children's meal.

Secondly, she also demonstrated astonishing faith. She recognised that a crumb of Jesus' power would suffice to deliver her daughter from whatever demonic oppression she suffered. A crumb of power attached to a seed of faith was enough, according to Jesus, to remove mountains! The mixing of metaphors suffices to show that a little goes a long way in the kingdom of God. Jesus was greatly impressed by her reply and by the faith and understanding that lay behind it. He gave the word for her daughter's deliverance.

Jesus has always been impressed by those with faith combined with boldness, and there is a long line of Christians down the years who bear witness to this; whether it is Jackie Pullinger stepping ashore in Hong Kong with almost no money in her pocket, but a strong sense of calling to go and minister in the Walled City (as it was then); or someone who has risked reputation or livelihood to tell of the love of God: the same combination of faith and boldness is the basis of their discipleship.

One missionary hero of mine from the nineteenth century is Fraser. A number of years ago, OMF published a short account of his work amongst the Lisu people in Northern China. Fraser is reported to have said, "There is a vast, vast field for us to go and claim by faith."

It was John Wimber who gave us the phrase that 'faith is spelt R-I-S-K'; and John Collins, with whom I worked at Holy Trinity Brompton, who often said that faith is 'daring to believe'. The Syro-Phoenician woman was (like the centurion) one of the earliest examples in the Gospels of an individual combining faith and boldness to a rare degree. Look at any work of God today: soon you will discover the same unchanging combination.

The challenge to us of this woman's faith is to 'step out of the boat', as Peter did, to walk towards Jesus on the water; to dare to believe God, and to lay hold of him and his promises and power with both hands. Remember that a crumb is enough!

The outcome of this meeting between Jesus and the woman was the deliverance of her daughter. Like some of the other healing miracles in the Gospels, it took place without Jesus being present with the patient: a word was given from afar, and she was made well. In this case, a demon was cast out and, when the woman returned, she found her daughter lying peacefully on her bed. Jesus had performed a miracle outside the borders of Israel, and, in so doing, had sent out a powerful signal that no one was excluded from the blessings of his kingdom. The Gentile mother's persistent confidence demonstrated that the love of God is not exclusive—it is for the whole world, and can be taken hold of by all who believe. The only person who is excluded is the one who excludes himself. Jesus came, as he himself said, 'not to condemn the world, but that the world might be saved through him'.

*Lord Jesus, you excluded no one from your kingdom who came to you in faith. May I not limit the extent of your love. May I go where you send me, say what you tell me, and do what you give me to do, with faith and love. Amen.*

# 9

# Liberation:
# The Gadarene Demoniac

## Patrick Whitworth

This story must rank as one of the most dramatic and disturbing in the ministry of Jesus. It follows one of the most endearing and attractive of Jesus' miracles, the calming of the storm, and it would be easy to pay less attention to this miracle which seems so out of our experience. Yet, unless we take a pair of scissors to the gospels and cut out all the uncomfortable teaching or disturbing miracles, we must face up to the full extent and range of Jesus' actions. To do anything other is simply to take the cosy bits and jettison those parts that challenge either our world-view or lifestyle. For most of us, this story is disturbing both to our outlook on life and to our ineffectiveness in dealing with the severely demonised. Once again we must carefully observe this extraordinary meeting and see what we can learn:

> They sailed to the region of the Gerasenes, which is across the lake from Galilee. When Jesus stepped ashore, he was met by a demon-possessed man from the town. For a long time this man had not worn clothes or lived in a house, but had lived in the tombs. When he saw Jesus, he cried out and fell at his feet, shouting at the top of his voice, "What do you want with me, Jesus, Son of the Most High God? I beg you, don't torture me!" For Jesus had commanded the evil spirit to come out of the man. Many times it had seized him, and though he was chained hand and foot and kept under guard, he had broken his chains and had been driven by the demon into solitary places.

Jesus asked him, "What is your name?"

"Legion," he replied, because many demons had gone into him. And they begged him repeatedly not to order them to go into the Abyss.

A large herd of pigs was feeding there on the hillside. The demons begged Jesus to let them go into them, and he gave them permission. When the demons came out of the man, they went into the pigs, and the herd rushed down the steep bank into the lake and was drowned.

When those tending the pigs saw what had happened, they ran off and reported this in the town and countryside, and the people went out to see what had happened. When they came to Jesus, they found the man from whom the demons had gone out, sitting at Jesus' feet, dressed and in his right mind; and they were afraid. Those who had seen it told the people how the demon-possessed man had been cured. Then all the people of the region of the Gerasenes asked Jesus to leave them, because they were overcome with fear. So he got into the boat and left.

The man from whom the demons had gone out begged to go with him, but Jesus sent him away, saying, "Return home and tell how much God has done for you." So the man went away and told all over town how much Jesus had done for him.

*Luke 8:26–39*

Jesus had arrived at the territory of the Gerasenes by boat. On the way over, the party had experienced a fierce storm, which was so severe that the disciples had feared for their lives. "Master, Master," they had cried out, "we're going to drown!" But Jesus had stood up in the boat and rebuked the wind and raging sea and the storm dramatically subsided. The incident ends with the disciples asking the searching question, "Who is this? He commands even the winds and the water, and they obey him." The disciples were soon to discover more of his authority in a very different theatre of action. However, there appears to be some link between the two incidents in that, through the use of the word 'rebuke' in the calming of the storm, it seems that Jesus perceived something malevolent in it—a malevolence that was to become far more obvious in the Gadarene demoniac. As soon as the boat came ashore, Jesus and the disciples were met by a man apparently more demonised than any other in the gospels. In looking now at this meeting, there are three aspects to focus on particularly: the reality of evil and demonisation; the authority of Jesus; and the price of liberation. We shall look at each in turn.

The world-view of the average first century Jew and the twenty first century westerner is vastly different in many respects; one of which is their respective view of evil. For us, today, the tendency is to sanitize evil and think of it as very unsocial behaviour, driven by uncivilised attitudes, which can be educated out of us. But the New Testament view is that evil can be traced to a source of infection which Jesus came into the world to destroy; that is, both its power and, in the end, its effect. John said that the reason the Son of God appeared in the world was 'to destroy the devil's work' (I John 3:8). The exorcisms carried out by Jesus signified that a real spiritual battle against Satan and his forces was underway. This kind of conflict was immediately comprehensible within the world-view of the first century A.D. It may be asked whether that world-view, which Jesus shared with his contemporaries, is still the right framework within which we can account for the manifest evil at work in the world today. We can maintain with confidence that it is both coherent and necessary, and makes sense of the evidence. How else do we explain that, as *The Times* reported last year, there are 100,000 practising witches in the UK, or that people who have been neighbours for years take part in orgies of violence in Rwanda, Bosnia and East Timor— unless we take into account that there is an evil power, Satan, who works on the weaknesses and prejudices of people? There is also the evidence of those who have particular ministries of deliverance today (an area which must be treated with great care and proper pastoral supervision). The ministry of Jesus teaches us that there is indeed deep underlying warfare going on between the kingdom of God and the dominion of Satan, in which the meeting with the Gadarene demoniac is but an individual incident. We must now look at this narrative a little more carefully.

As with many of these Gospel meetings, the authority of Jesus is clearly evident throughout. The encounter takes place as soon as Jesus steps ashore from the boat. The effect of demonisation in this man is soon apparent. He has no dignity or self respect, so is wearing no clothes. He has no normal social relationships, so having no home. He is unhealthily obsessed with death, so is living in the local cemetery and moving amongst the tombs. He had an unnatural strength, which meant that he was bound hand and foot with chains, from which he sometimes broke free. He was often driven into isolation. In fact, he shows all the worst hallmarks of the work of the devil, about which Jesus warned his disciples when he said, "The thief [meaning the devil] comes only to steal and kill and destroy; I [Jesus] have come that they may have life, and have it to the full" (John 10:10). Never was this contrast more graphically illustrated than in this meeting with the Gadarene demoniac. The man's dignity, clothes, home and relationships had been stolen, he was fascinated with death and was being destroyed. In an extreme form, the like of which only very rarely occurs, he manifested the disintegration that comes with the unfettered presence of the devil, but now those effects and presence were to be gloriously reversed.

The authority and person of Jesus was immediately recognised by the demoniac: "What do you want with me, Jesus, Son of the Most High God? I beg you don't torture me!" Here was no meeting of two equal and opposite forces, but the admission by the devils infesting this man of complete impotence before the superior power of Jesus. This is an important point to grasp because the Church has sometimes got into the habit of thinking that—and, more frequently, acting as though—spiritual warfare, whether on an individual or collective scale, is a struggle of two equal and opposite forces. This was the teaching of the Manichees, who had so influenced Augustine before his conversion. From the moment the evil spirits recognised Jesus, they were literally at his mercy.

At this point, Jesus, addressing the demonised man, asks his name. A number of reasons have been put forward as to why he did so at this point. Some say it is to gain power over the evil spirits before commanding them to depart; some that it was the first step in the exorcism; but perhaps the simplest reason is overlooked, namely Jesus' desire to form a relationship with this man, whose identity had been lost in the appalling effects of the demonisation. However, the man is unable to give his own name and, instead, shows by his answer that his own identity has been overwhelmed by the presence of what seems like a legion of devils who have come to destroy his identity and personality! In fact, in a legion there could be up to six thousand soldiers. The admission of the scale of the problem having been made, we come to the moment of liberation!

Last night I settled down to watch the feature film *Star Wars* with our young son. I thoroughly enjoyed it and remarked that I could see a good Ph.D in the making, entitled 'The influence of Alice in Wonderland on the makers of Star Wars'! He was not amused by such a fogey-ish remark! In the film there is a climax when Jedi takes on the arch-enemy, Darth Maul, who is eventually defeated by the Jedi's apprentice. At the moment of Darth Maul's destruction, he plunges into an abyss. I wondered whether the makers of the film realised how like the biblical account of the destiny of demons the fate of Darth Maul was! The abyss to which these demons refer in the Gospel is that place of final imprisonment to which they will be sent. (See Revelation 20:1–3.) They begged not to be sent into the Abyss and did so repeatedly. Here we come to a moment of mystery in this meeting: why did Jesus not either destroy them or send them into the Abyss; surely they deserved no less! Instead Jesus acceded to their request, sending them into a herd of swine grazing nearby and close to the sea, bringing about their destruction in that way.

The fate of the swine has troubled Western Christians. 'Surely,' we say, 'Jesus got it wrong. He should have sent the demons to the Abyss and refused to allow them to destroy the herd.' What could be his reasons for allowing the demons to enter the swine? A number of answers have been put forward. Firstly, to an orthodox Jew, a herd of swine was unclean and so was worthy of little respect; so to send demons into swine would be like permitting rats to run into refuse—hardly something to be too concerned about! Another reason (suggested by a local guide to a group of our parishioners whilst travelling in that part of Galilee) was that the pigs were used in local pagan worship, so to permit their destruction was to curtail that cultic activity. Or it could be to demonstrate to the locals, to the herdsmen and to the disciples the extent both of the demoniac's possession and the scale of the deliverance which Jesus so powerfully accomplished in this miracle. Of all the explanations, this is the one I prefer. After all, the destruction of the herd shows in a highly dramatic and visual way: the scale of this man's infestation, the true destructive nature of the demons, the power and authority of Christ, and the value that Jesus placed on one man's liberation which was worth more than a herd of pigs! Naturally, we do feel sorry for the pigs who lost their lives and the farmers who lost much of their livelihood, but Jesus is not fettered in his action either by regard for the local economy or for the lives of these animals.

It is a curious state of affairs that at the end of the encounter the locals were more afraid of Jesus, the liberator, than they had been of the victim, to whom they had grown accustomed. We are told by Luke that 'all the people of the region of the Gerasenes asked ['begged' in Mark's account] Jesus to leave because they were overcome with fear.' The reaction of the local people is a commentary on the fact that we can often accommodate ourselves to the familiar, however terrible it may be, rather than face up to the challenge of having our working assumptions challenged by Jesus. We are reminded that many people today prefer to entertain a picture of Jesus without supernatural power: an image we can keep at a safe distance, whether in stained glass, tradition or empty ritual.

However, a remarkable and deeply disconcerting event had taken place; the demoniac now meekly sat at Jesus' feet 'clothed and in his right mind', a large herd of pigs lay drowned in the Sea of Galilee, and the people could either enquire further of this Jesus, who had come amongst them, or hope that he would go quickly without further incident. As we have seen, they hoped for a quick exit by Jesus. And he obliged them, knowing as he himself had said elsewhere that, "If I drive out demons by the finger of God, then the kingdom of God has come to you." The kingdom had come among them, but they were not ready for its potent presence.

However one man, and he the most unlikely, was ready for use in the kingdom of God: the Gadarene ex-demoniac. We have no other name for him. He begged to go with Jesus! And interestingly, although Jesus permitted the demons to go into the pigs when they too "begged" him, he would not allow this ex-demoniac to go with him. Why? Because he was to be the link between Jesus and this traumatised community. His place was now amongst them to explain what had happened. He was given the explicit instruction by Jesus to, "return home and tell how much God has done for you." One imagines that his talks were the biggest thing in town for many years to come!

This fascinating and remarkable meeting is the account of one man's liberation by the power and authority of Jesus. It is also a clear example of the deliverance ministry which Jesus passed on to the Church. When Jesus later commissioned the apostles to teach new disciples, "everything I have commanded you" (see Matthew 28:18), the expulsion of demons was definitely part of it. After all, earlier in Matthew's Gospel these same disciples had been sent out by Jesus to, "preach this message: The kingdom of heaven is near. Heal the sick, raise the dead, cleanse those who have leprosy, drive out demons." Since, therefore, Jesus had included the expulsion of demons in his commands to them, they were now to instruct new disciples to continue this ministry.

But how is this ministry of Christ to be carried on in the early twenty-first century? An article in *The Times* by the religious correspondent Ruth Gledhill, was catchily headed: *'Deliver us from illicit exorcisms,' Bishops plead.* There is no doubt that most denominations find that this ministry of deliverance is more prevalent. This increase is in the context of two world–views that now compete for our attention. One is based on the rational, in which there is little scope for supernatural intervention of any kind, and in which 'professionals' operate in a highly regulated world, where patients are treated with a combination of drugs and therapy. The other world-view is based on 'spirit': it is romantic, post-modern and increasingly pagan—and a complete contrast to the computer dominated technology of our age. In the context of these two competing world-views, the Church must hold faithfully to a gospel which has power to deliver us from evil, and which is both supernatural and reasonable. This is not the place to give a practical and pastoral account of how the Church can follow the example of Jesus in this encounter. But we can reiterate some of the values that should guide us: belief in the power of Jesus to deliver from evil; love for the individual who needs deliverance; consultation and communication with those in leadership in the Church; deep intercession and prayer for all those concerned; and an unshakeable confidence in the supernatural power of Jesus.

For ourselves, let us pray that Christ may free us from all evil, and give us the strength to resist the disintegrating effect of the devil's work, remembering Peter's salutary advice:

Be self-controlled and alert. Your enemy the devil prowls around like a roaring lion looking for someone to devour. Resist him, standing firm in the faith, because you know that your brothers throughout the world are undergoing the same kind of sufferings.

And the God of all grace, who called you to his eternal glory in Christ, after you have suffered a little while, will himself restore you and make you strong, firm and steadfast. To him be the power for ever and ever. Amen.

*I Peter 5:8–11*

*Lord Jesus, who drove from this man the demons that controlled him, drive far from us all manner of evil, through the power of your presence; keep us in your peace, and give us sure confidence in the power of your name and your blood to defeat all the works of the enemy. May we sit at your feet, then go and tell of what you have done for us. Amen.*

# 10

# Invitation:
# The Rich Young Ruler

## *Patrick Whitworth*

What is becoming evident in these meetings with Jesus is that Jesus was able to go to the heart of the matter very quickly. Never was this more the case than in the meeting of the rich young ruler with Jesus. In just a few moments of conversation, you feel this endearing young man being weighed, tested and found wanting! It is a revealing conversation.

> As Jesus started on his way, a man ran up to him and fell on his knees before him. "Good teacher," he asked, "what must I do to inherit eternal life?"
> "Why do you call me good?" Jesus answered. "No one is good—except God alone. You know the commandments: 'Do not murder, do not commit adultery, do not steal, do not give false testimony, do not defraud, honour your father and mother.'"
> "Teacher," he declared, "all these I have kept since I was a boy."
> Jesus looked at him and loved him. "One thing you lack," he said. "Go, sell everything you have and give to the poor, and you will have treasure in heaven. Then come, follow me."
> At this the man's face fell. He went away sad, because he had great wealth.
> Jesus looked around and said to his disciples, "How hard it is for the rich to enter the kingdom of God!"
> The disciples were amazed at his words. But Jesus said again, "Children, how hard it is to enter the kingdom of God. It is easier for a camel to go through the eye of a needle than for a rich man to enter the kingdom of God."

The disciples were even more amazed, and said to each other, "Who then can be saved?"

Jesus looked at them and said, "With man this is impossible, but not with God; all things are possible with God."

Peter said to him, "We have left everything to follow you!"

"I tell you the truth," Jesus replied, "no one who has left home or brothers or sisters or mother or father or children or fields for me and the gospel will fail to receive a hundred times as much in this present age (homes, brothers, sisters, mothers, children and fields— and with them, persecutions) and in the age to come, eternal life. But many who are first will be last, and the last first."

*Mark 10:17–31*

There are four parts to this encounter: a question, an answer, an observation, and an interjection. Little is given away about the identity of this young ruler. The incident is recorded in all three synoptic Gospels. Luke's version is the longest; typically, Mark's account is the most dynamic. In Mark's Gospel, the young ruler throws himself at Jesus' feet, and later we are told that Jesus 'loved' him which is, to say the least, an unusual statement about Jesus' reaction to someone. The young man, possibly a late teenager or in his early twenties, was pious, earnest and forthright. He comes directly to the point, asking Jesus a question he must have been thinking about for some time.

The question was a good one: "Good teacher, what must I do to inherit eternal life?" But, as so often with conversations with Jesus, he would not get his answer on a plate. There would be plenty of issues to consider along the way. The terms in which the question had been asked are worth looking at, for they contain the clues to the way this man was thinking, and help us to understand the way in which Jesus responded to him. So let us examine the question a little more closely. Implied in the question is the notion that if I 'do' certain things, then this prize of eternal life will be mine. Presumably, the man thought that he had only to meet some qualification, and then 'eternal life' would be his! He was earnest and sincere in his request. Mark tells us both that he 'ran' up to Jesus, and then 'knelt before him', so he certainly did not let any pomposity or self-regard get in the way of finding an answer to the question which troubled him. Nevertheless, his approach concerned 'doing' things in order to acquire eternal life. It was this aspect of his thinking which Jesus was to pursue and expose. I suspect that this rich young ruler, presumably having inherited his wealth, now wanted to hear what were the conditions upon which he could inherit eternal life and therefore what he should 'do' to fulfil those conditions. If this was what was in the man's mind, you can almost hear Jesus thinking, 'If you want to go down that route let us see how far we get.'

From the outset, Jesus questioned this man's terms. Notice that Jesus picks him up on the adjective 'good', making the point that only God is good—so why was he calling Jesus 'good'; thus making the man think further about the identity of the one he was addressing. From this rather exacting response to the young man's question, it was clear that his simple request would lead to demands of which he had not dreamed! Jesus then proceeds in a thoroughly orthodox way along the route mapped out by the young ruler's question. If 'eternal life' was to be gained by 'doing', it could only be through perfect obedience to the commandments, so Jesus then goes down a familiar path, saying to him, "You know the commandments", choosing those that fall into the love-of-neighbour category. Keep these, Jesus implies, to which the young man blithely replies: "All these I have kept since I was a boy." It is in this reply that the young man betrays both his naivety and his charm, which must have endeared him so much to Jesus. In all probability, the young man could not call to mind any glaring examples of failing to keep these commands—not, at least, in deed. He had not murdered, nor committed adultery; he could not recall deliberately telling a 'whopper', and he had excellent relations with his parents—perhaps his father had died, anyway. But, of course, he may not have heard Jesus' teaching in the Sermon on the Mount, in which he extended the scope of the commandments to cover not just deeds but also words and thoughts. If the young ruler had been sitting on the mountainside when Jesus applied the prohibitions of the commandments to word and thought, his reply, hopefully, would have been very different. Indeed, he would have heard Jesus' words at the end of a section of teaching, in which he said, 'Be perfect, as your heavenly Father is perfect.' But the young man was remarkably confident of his righteousness. Jesus did not question his own self-assessment, but must have smiled inwardly before placing an almost insurmountable roadblock on this young man's smooth path to eternal life.

Jesus issued a demand that stopped the young man in his tracks when he said: 'Go, sell everything you have and give to the poor, and you will have treasure in heaven. Then come, follow me.' The question that we must ask is why did Jesus make the obstacle so high for this man to jump? Why did Jesus ask him to do something so difficult that the young man declined? The answer might be that for the man this challenge was a moment of revelation; a moment of crisis; a moment of deep spiritual instruction.

We will look at each of these in turn. It was a moment of revelation. Until then he was a blithe spirit, we should say, glad and confident—and no doubt that was attractive, if unreal. Jesus' demand that he should sell up and follow him was, I am sure, designed to show him where his heart lay; for the way Jesus speaks to him reminds us of some other words he spoke, in the Sermon on the Mount: "Do not store up for yourselves treasures on earth... but store up for yourselves treasures in heaven." The point is that without grace at work in this young man's soul it would be very hard for him to sell up. Although he had been able to say glibly that he had followed the commandments, he suddenly found that he could not so easily give his riches to the poor; indeed, he found that he was more attached to his wealth than he had realized. It was, therefore, a moment of revelation to him when he discovered what his true desires were, and that moment of revelation made him sorrowful. Suddenly, the motives of his heart had been revealed. It was a sad moment!

It was also a moment of crisis. By this I mean that it was a moment of critical choice. 'Crisis' is generally a time of intense choice. The choice was whether to sell up, and then follow Jesus as one of his disciples—or to return to his property and care for his possessions. We know that he decided to do the latter. The reason why he chose this course of action brings us to the hub of the encounter. This moment was one of deep spiritual instruction. Already, we have seen that it was a moment of revelation and crisis—but it was also an answer to his original question. The young man had asked, 'What must I do to inherit eternal life?' As we observed, Jesus took him down the traditional Jewish route of obeying the commandments and the young man had gladly followed; more than that, he had said that he had observed the commandments from his youth. What the young ruler had to learn was that 'no-one will be declared righteous in his [God's] sight by observing the law; rather, through the law we become conscious of sin' (Romans 3:20). In fact, our young ruler had been assured of his goodness rather than convicted of his failures, when he observed his life in the light of the commandments. So Jesus sought to show him the true nature of his heart, and its poverty, despite his self assurance. He did this by giving him a test which could only be surmounted by grace.

In essence, the spiritual instruction we are given through this incident is that God's grace can do in us what observation of the law could never do. Let me explain. The young ruler found that he could not sell up his property and follow Jesus. He could not do that because his inheritance meant more to him than following Jesus. He had a desire to do his duty but this, in fact, fell far short of either enabling him to obey the commandments fully (in thought as well as in deed) or providing him with sufficient motivation to sell his riches and follow Jesus—only grace could have done this.

In Luke 18, we find that three stories are systematically grouped together which more or less make the same point. The first of these stories is the parable of the Pharisee and the tax collector. The Pharisee was attempting to gain eternal life by his religious duties of fasting, giving and tithing, whereas the tax collector had failed miserably, and admitted it. Jesus said that the tax-collector went home 'justified' (or assured of the gift of eternal life). The next story is of Jesus rebuking the disciples who were turning away little children who wanted to touch him. Jesus said that 'anyone who will not receive the kingdom of God like a little child will never enter it.' So the kingdom of God is entered, or the gift of eternal life is received, through simple trust. This was the lesson that the disciples needed to know; which those who were confident in their own righteousness needed to know; and which the rich young ruler needed to know. It was the same lesson for all, namely that we enter the kingdom by grace—and receive eternal life by grace. This term 'grace' implies that God treats us as we do not deserve. His love for us does not depend on what we have or have not done: he deals with us according to his grace. This was the piece of profound spiritual instruction that the young ruler needed to grasp, and he could only do so when he realised that he could not inherit eternal life by following the commandments. He thought he could, until Jesus challenged him with something which was way beyond his capability. When he realised this, he was sad. But this sadness could have become a springboard to diving into God's grace: perhaps it was!

It is worth pointing out that selling everything is not a condition for discipleship. In this case, Jesus was challenging the young ruler to do something in his own strength, which he knew the young ruler could not do without asking for his help—without his grace working in his life. However, what we see from the next chapter in Luke, in the course of Jesus' meeting with Zacchaeus, is that restitution of illicit gain is definitely a result of discipleship. We are shown that the work of grace—acceptance and forgiveness—enables Zacchaeus to give away a large slice of his wealth. Nevertheless, Jesus uses the reaction of the ruler here to make a general point about the effects of wealth on becoming a disciple. Jesus said 'How hard it is for the rich to enter the kingdom of God! Indeed, it is easier for a camel to go through the eye of a needle than for a rich man to enter the kingdom of God.'

The pursuits of power, sex and money are still the three biggest hurdles to people's entry into the kingdom. Each has a power to hold us from entering the kingdom. Here, Jesus was acknowledging the power of money. In I Timothy, Paul wrote that 'the love of money is a root of all kinds of evil'. Money, like so many of God's gifts, is morally neutral, but it can soon enslave us. If we make it our object in life, it is easy to become hardened in its pursuit, arrogant in its possession, and self-advertising in its use. For these and other reasons, it is hard for a rich person to enter the kingdom of God. The reason for this is simply that getting it, keeping it and spending it becomes all consuming, and then God seems like an intrusion on what we think is our own rightful kingdom. Of course, this does not mean that rich, or very rich, people cannot be Christians; it does mean that they may have to exercise more vigilance over their souls. They may need to pray for greater sensitivity and humility in their lives. They will certainly have to learn the twin responsibilities of generosity in giving and faithfulness in stewardship. All this is possible through God's grace but, nonetheless, Jesus says it can be hard. This was Jesus' main observation on the meeting with the rich young ruler and, when those around Jesus heard what he had to say about the difficulties for rich people entering the kingdom, they rather desperately asked, 'who can be saved?' Jesus then gave us the clue to his power and grace, saying, "What is impossible with men is possible with God." Surely this is a reference to the grace of God which is shown in the cross. Perhaps, therefore, it is no coincidence that Jesus goes on to speak about the cross immediately after this encounter with the young ruler. "We are going up to Jerusalem... and the Son of Man will be turned over to the Gentiles. They will mock him, insult him, spit on him, flog him, and kill him. On the third day he will rise again." Luke's juxtaposition of this saying with the three previous stories, which are all about the need to enter God's kingdom by grace, is no coincidence. It is his way of showing that what is impossible to us is only made possible by understanding the action of Jesus on the cross. As Luther once said, to understand Christianity we must begin with the wounds of Christ.

Finally, we must consider Peter's interjection: 'We have left all to follow you.' Why did Peter say this? Was it a plea for some recognition that he, together with some of the other disciples, had already left their livelihood to follow Jesus—and he wanted Jesus to acknowledge this? Was it a statement that sought to correct Jesus, because they had left their business and so had proved that such actions were not impossible? Or was it a plea for some reward for their sacrifice? Whatever thought prompted Peter's interjection, Jesus uses his reply to make a solemn announcement about all those who sacrifice either family or wealth for the kingdom of God. They will receive blessings in this life and in the age to come: 'eternal life'. The blessings in this life will not necessarily be material but more likely spiritual, and such faith, enabled by grace, will be rewarded by eternal life.

Jesus has now answered the young ruler's question. To inherit eternal life you need grace, leading to faith, expressing itself in sacrifice, which will bring blessings in this life, and possibly persecutions. (See Mark 10:30.) It was another memorable meeting, with important teaching. So the young ruler went away sad. Since we are told that Jesus loved him, you cannot help wondering whether, after the death and resurrection of Jesus, grace was released in that young man—and his riches placed at the disposal of the kingdom. I like to think so!

*Lord Jesus, release in me your gift of grace, that I may have the faith to offer up to you not only my heart but all that I have been given: my family, my friends, my income and my wealth. Keep me sensitive to the needs of others, generous in my response and humble in my stewardship of all I have been given. Amen.*

# 11

# Deception:
# The Woman Caught in Adultery

## Patrick Whitworth

St. John wrote, 'If we claim to be without sin, we deceive ourselves and the truth is not in us' [1 John 1:8]. Until Jesus demonstrated this central spiritual principle to the Pharisees, who had dragged the dishevelled and distraught woman to his feet, they were guilty of a most notable case of deception. But that is to jump in at the conclusion of this meeting, which we now consider in its entirety. The Gospel of John is the only one to include it.

At dawn he appeared again in the temple courts, where all the people gathered around him, and he sat down to teach them. The teachers of the law and the Pharisees brought in a woman caught in adultery. They made her stand before the group and said to Jesus, "Teacher, this woman was caught in the act of adultery. In the Law Moses commanded us to stone such women. Now what do you say?" They were using this question as a trap, in order to have a basis for accusing him.

But Jesus bent down and started to write on the ground with his finger. When they kept on questioning him, he straightened up and said to them, "If any one of you is without sin, let him be the first to throw a stone at her." Again he stooped down and wrote on the ground.

At this, those who heard began to go away one at a time, the older ones first, until only Jesus was left, with the woman still standing there. Jesus straightened up and asked her, "Woman, where are they? Has no one condemned you?"

"No one, sir," she said.

"Then neither do I condemn you," Jesus declared. "Go now and leave your life of sin."

*John 8:2–11*

There is an obvious three-stage development to this encounter. At the outset, the Pharisees plainly intended to place Jesus on the horns of a dilemma from which, they thought, he could not extract himself without discrediting his ministry and teaching. But with a single challenge, which went to the very heart of the Pharisees' moral life, Jesus then effectively turned the tables on the woman's accusers. Finally, Jesus summons the woman to a new way of life— which is Jesus' answer to the question he had originally been asked. So Jesus proved in action what he had said: that he had not come to condemn the world but to rescue it. It is now time to look a little more closely at the issues raised in this meeting, which have a particular importance to our own generation.

On many occasions in the Gospels, the Pharisees came to Jesus with the specific intention of discrediting his teaching by showing that it was in contravention of the Law of Moses, or was disloyal to the Jewish nation. A well known instance of this is the time the Pharisees brought a denarius to Jesus, asking whether it was lawful to pay taxes to Caesar. We know the magisterial answer Jesus gave to that test question: "Give to Caesar what is Caesar's, and to God what is God's" (Matthew 22:21b.) On another occasion, an expert in the Law asked Jesus what he considered to be the greatest commandment. Jesus gave as his reply the summary of the Law which we now know as the two great commandments. The Sadducees came with a test question which was notoriously contrived, and was intended to disprove the possibility of the resurrection, which they believed did not occur. (See Matthew 22:23). In reply to their question, Jesus roundly told them they did not know either the Scriptures or the power of God, which must have sent them either scurrying back to their scrolls or, more likely, to devise a contest with him in which they could more readily control the outcome. Of course, all of these test questions were sub-plots to a deadly power play, in which the various parties contended for the allegiance of the people. Ultimately, the people could only follow one leader, who would hold sway over them.

But this test question was given greater drama and potency by having a live embodiment of the moral and spiritual issues at stake. It is therefore a highly charged occasion. It is quite possible that the woman whom the Pharisees brought to the seated Jesus was a prostitute. Some have said that she was Mary Magdalene, though there is no evidence for this. In any event, the Pharisees were not averse to being 'peeping-toms' in order to catch the couple 'in flagrante', and they were highly selective in choosing to bring along the woman as their moral exhibit—not the man or both of them! It was carefully and cleverly planned to heighten the confrontation they sought with Jesus and to highlight the dilemma that faced him. If Jesus did not condemn her for her flagrant and undeniable sin, he would show that he did not follow the teaching of Moses, and so could be specifically branded a heretic. On the other hand, if Jesus upheld the punishment laid down in Mosaic Law, then he would seemingly be abandoning his teaching of grace—teaching that so exasperated the Pharisees, led him to keep the company of tax-collectors and sinners, and lay at the heart of his instruction about the kingdom of God. At last they had a defining moment which Jesus could not avoid, and one which would lead to the discrediting of his teaching—or so they thought! In a few moments the tables would be truly turned!

John has already told us that, as was customary amongst rabbis, Jesus was seated to teach the people. He was in the Temple precincts, surrounded by a crowd of people, so this meeting —or confrontation—was in a highly public situation, which was as the Pharisees wished it to be. They wanted plenty of witnesses to hear what they hoped would be an incriminating reply by Jesus, which would be the prelude to a religious prosecution against him, and his public humiliation. So it was through the crowd, in the Temple courts, that the Pharisees dragged this humiliated woman to the seated Jesus. They threw down their 'religious gauntlet' and waited triumphantly for Jesus' confusion. Only a few moments and they would have the evidence necessary to begin formal proceedings against him, which would end his hold over the people and confirm their power. No doubt more than one Pharisee would have had his hands on his garments, ready to tear them in horror at the anticipated reply, and in relief that Jesus' threat to their hegemony was passing. But, for a time, Jesus did not reply. The posture of Jesus, and his physical actions, appear to be important to John for, on receiving their 'test question', John records that, "Jesus bent down and started to write on the ground with his finger" — and he did so for quite a while, for during this time the Pharisees kept on questioning him, cajoling him for a reply.

You may wonder why Jesus spent these moments writing with

his finger in the dust: what he was writing, and what was going through his mind—questions that give preachers plenty of scope for elaboration, but which must remain speculative. However, you can be sure that he knew in a flash what the Pharisees were up to; that he could see into the soul of the woman; and that he knew the crowd were waiting to hear his reply; and, almost to heighten the significance of what he was about to say, he kept them all waiting! Then one of the most famous replies in the Gospel rang out from his lips—for his hearers then, and for every succeeding generation. "If anyone of you is without sin, let him be the first to throw a stone at her," was Jesus' unexpected answer. The tables had been turned. Now, far from Jesus being tested, they were! You can imagine the crowd, as at Wimbledon, turning their heads to see what the Pharisees would now do with such a searching and scorching return!

I wonder what you consider to be the most vital word in Jesus' reply. It is probably a choice between the words "without" and "first". For me it is the little word "first". To understand this, you must appreciate the nature of stoning. It is not something most of us, thankfully, will ever have witnessed, although once, while walking through an ultra-conservative area of Jerusalem on the Sabbath, I experienced having a few lads throw pebbles at me! The point is that stoning is not like a firing squad, where a group of disciplined soldiers fire simultaneously at the prisoner. The firing squad act in unison, thereby mitigating, to some degree, the sense of personal involvement. Moreover, members of a firing squad act on the command of an officer, who in turn is executing the order of a court. But when it came to stoning this woman, the Pharisees would have been acting according to the Law of Moses, and the punishment laid down in it, but also would have been declaring themselves innocent of any sin; for Jesus' challenge to each of them was that the one who judged himself to be without sin should throw the *first* stone. Such a challenge to declare your innocence by throwing the first stone was not going to be met easily. No doubt the Pharisees would have spent a few moments in embarrassed silence, as each looked to the other to declare himself guiltless by throwing the first stone. But no one did, and we are told that the older and more senior Pharisees present recognised that they themselves had fallen into the trap designed for Jesus; and that, in all honesty, they could not meet his challenge of being without sin. John tells us that those who heard began to go away one at a time, the older ones first, until only Jesus was left, with the woman still standing there.

So we are presented with a final poignant scene in this meeting with Jesus. John tells us that while the Pharisees were slinking away, Jesus remained seated, head bowed, looking at the ground and writing in the dust with his finger. In his painting of this encounter, entitled *Jesus and the Adulterous Woman*, which hangs in the National Gallery, Rembrandt has all the light falling on the figure of the kneeeling woman, before a standing Christ. In the painting, Jesus casts a searching look at the woman. Although not entirely true to John's account, this serves to highlight the dramatic nature of the meeting.

Finally, Jesus looked up and addressed the woman, "Woman, where are they? Has no one condemned you?" Jesus could not have been too surprised that there was no one left, stone in hand, ready to hurl it at her. The wind had truly been taken from their sails. But Jesus now said these words, which held as great a significance for the woman as his earlier words of challenge had for the Pharisees. If Jesus' earlier words to the Pharisees had shown them their deepest spiritual problem, namely to recognise and admit their own need of grace, his words to the woman addressed her deepest spiritual need: namely for forgiveness, and a new way of life. As always in the New Testament, receiving grace must lead on to a new way of life. It is these words that are so important to us, too.

There are, of course, two sides to Jesus' pronouncement to the woman. The first part is a declaration; the second is a command. The declaration was that, along with the Pharisees who had now slunk away, he would not condemn her. But, unlike the Pharisees, Jesus, who was indeed without sin, had the right to pass judgment over her. But he chose not to condemn, but to forgive. The pedant might say that there was no verbal confession of guilt by the woman, which should precede her forgiveness; the answer to such an objection must be that Jesus knew very well the desire of her heart for forgiveness, and so pronounced it. This declaration of forgiveness to the woman takes us to the very centre of the gospel. It is a gospel of grace, which means that Jesus does not treat us according to what we deserve. The woman was given a glorious pardon. Here, Jesus was acting out what he had previously said, namely that "God did not send his Son into the world to condemn the world, but to save the world through him". So at the very centre of God's self-revelation in Jesus there is, as ever, forgiveness—coupled with transforming grace.

Jesus said to the woman: "Then neither do I condemn you.... Go now and leave your life of sin." Consider the second part of Jesus' declaration, "go now and leave your life of sin."—Here is the rub! But here, also, is the truth of God's grace through Jesus. His grace has the power, not only to forgive, but also to change. This change results from a combination of both the supernatural power of God and the will of the individual to change. For this woman, the effect of experiencing such forgiveness would be a desire to change her lifestyle; to leave her 'life of sin'. This challenge to the woman can easily be either overlooked or uncoupled from the gracious declaration that precedes it. Jesus' words to her are a significant reminder to our own generation not to uncouple what Jesus has put together. The Church is in a vulnerable position in this regard. Christians are in a minority in present day Britain. Wherever possible, the Church is to welcome people who are outside its fellowship; it needs to be free of all taint of self-righteousness; it wants to present itself as gracious and uncensorious, but in so doing it can jettison all boundaries. However, the fact is that God has set boundaries in the moral law, as expressed in the Ten Commandments—and to live grace-filled lives those commands should be followed. The temptation in recent years has been for parts of the Church to say, 'cleave but don't leave'; that is, enjoy the grace and forgiveness of God, but don't leave what is ungracious and unlawful in the sight of God. It is a truism about God's work that, whilst he accepts us as he finds us, he does not leave us—or want to leave us—as we were!

Jesus had an appropriate word for all. The Pharisees have a hard lesson on self-righteousness. They came to trap Jesus, but were themselves unmasked, and had to admit as much—to each other, to Jesus, to the woman and to the crowd—in effect admitting that they were by no means faultless. They slunk away, to nurse their bruised pride. Jesus had shown them that they had been victims of the self-deception that they were guiltless. They were in no position to judge and, for the same reason, neither are we. We have to confess that, often, we are as blind to ourselves as they were. There was a word for the poor woman: a word of free forgiveness, coupled to a command to leave what was degrading and contrary to God's revealed law. All were words of grace, and we find that, often, we ourselves need to hear and receive them. In a few sentences, in between doodling on the ground, Jesus had changed people's lives for good.

*Living Lord Jesus Christ, whose words are food to our lives, transform the poverty of our nature by the riches of your grace; help us to see ourselves as you do; to receive your undeserved forgiveness and, in your strength, to leave the ways that make us less than you intended us to be. Amen.*

# 12

# Adoration:
# Mary—The Woman with Perfume

## *Jon Soper*

---

This is a meeting that has much to teach us about the nature of true worship.

Following the raising of Lazarus, the Jewish leaders and elders were thrown into consternation and wanted to kill Jesus, so he moved to a region near the desert (see John11:54). Then he decides to return towards Jerusalem, arriving in Bethany again with his friends Lazarus (newly back to life), Mary and Martha. It is only six days before the Passover and a few days before Jesus is going to die. A dinner is given by them in Jesus' honour. Lazarus is reclining there, with Jesus and a number of others.

> Then Mary took about a pint of pure nard, an expensive perfume; she poured it on Jesus' feet and wiped his feet with her hair. And the house was filled with the fragrance of the perfume.
>
> But one of his disciples, Judas Iscariot, who was later to betray him, objected, "Why wasn't this perfume sold and the money given to the poor? It was worth a year's wages." He did not say this because he cared about the poor but because he was a thief; as keeper of the money bag, he used to help himself to what was put into it.
>
> "Leave her alone," Jesus replied. "It was intended that she should save this perfume for the day of my burial. You will always have the poor among you, but you will not always have me."
>
> *John 12:3–8*

Martha is serving the meal, and in this case she does not seem to get anxious and fretful about doing all the serving while Mary worships. John presents her as somebody who is now, after the raising of her brother, much more content to serve Jesus. It is then that Mary carries out an extraordinary action, something right out of the blue. Her pint of pure nard is an incredibly expensive quantity of the perfume, as we know from the comment of Judas that its cost was equivalent to a year's wages. If you had a pint of something costing a year's salary, you would treat it very carefully indeed! Mary decides that now is the time to use this expensive perfume. In doing this she is trying to express her gratitude for what Jesus has done for Lazarus, and in her own life. One of the features of worship is that singing, clapping, weeping or simply being silent is often an outward expression of what is going on inside. And that is what Mary is doing now—expressing outwardly a deep sense of gratitude for what she feels within.

Taking the bottle and pouring it over Jesus' feet, as he reclined there was an extraordinary action to perform whilst they were all eating. It was also a very humble action; oil or perfume is normally poured on the head, but she felt that she would pour it over his feet. Foot care was normally the preserve of servants; when John the Baptist said that there was one coming after him whose sandals he was not worthy to untie, that was an astonishing statement. Only servants untied sandals, and he was saying that he was not even worthy to be a servant. So Mary was, in effect, declaring to Jesus that she was his grateful servant, and she gave everything. In pouring it out, she is expressing extravagant devotion. It is not just a little dab and rub, indeed it does not matter if it spills on the ground (there go January's and February's wages down into the gutter!) It is a big splash, all over his feet. She wants to give what she has, unreservedly.

Mary is also extremely careless of her reputation: she does not mind how her action looks to others. Women who let their hair down in those days were seen as prostitutes. She wanted to dry Jesus' feet with her hair: a totally uninhibited action. Nor does she say anything. It is almost as though her action were beyond words, issuing from the very depths of her being.

Mary is truly reverent, humble, and intimate with Jesus. Wiping his feet with her hair is an intimate action. Jesus accepts it; he does not pull his feet away, saying, 'No, no; that is inappropriate.' Mary's actions convey an attitude that should govern our worship, both together in our churches and when we are on our own. On the one hand there is *reverence*, because he is God Almighty and he is our Lord; and, on the other, there is *intimacy*, because he is the friend of sinners, our Lover—the one who can be closer to us than anyone else we can know.

Women in the Bible often teach us about worship. In Matthew 28, after Jesus has been raised from the dead, the women are looking for him. He comes to them and says, "Greetings," whereupon they fall at his feet and worship him. In the action of bowing down before Jesus and clasping his feet, we see again those twin attitudes of reverence and intimacy. We may lean more towards one than the other: we may like to be very reverent and full of awe before God, because that is the way we see him, or we might like to be very friendly and intimate with God. God definitely wants us to be both reverent and intimate in our worship of him.

John tells us that, as this act of adoration takes place, the house is filled with the fragrance of the perfume. As we worship Jesus, there is not usually a fragrance in the physical sense, but there is a sense of the glory of God, and of joy and love expressed on people's faces. As we draw close to God, the 'fragrance of Jesus' fills the place (whether spiritually or physically), filling our hearts.

But for some it is not a wonderful thing, because the fragrance of Jesus does divide people. If you are a Christian, and you love Jesus, the fragrance of Jesus is delightful, but for others it is more of a stench. As Mary pours out the perfume, to Judas it is like a stench. He sees it first of all as a waste—why pour this expensive perfume on Jesus when the money it cost could have been used for the poor? In a sense it appears to be a very 'correct' attitude, but John reveals a bit of the psychology of Judas, showing us that he is not really thinking about the poor at all, but that he wants to take the money because he is a thief.

Adoration and worship are criticised by some as being a waste. They point out that we spend lots of time just singing songs to Jesus or bowing down before him or praying to him. Judas' case is that the extravagant forms of worship are immoral and wrong. In our culture, that kind of abandoned, generous worship can seem obsessive; as people observe Christians who are obviously delighted and full of joy in Jesus, they describe what is happening as being a bit 'over the top' or 'happy-clappy', simply because they do not know for themselves the reality of the love that Christians have for Jesus. Worship—the adoration of Jesus—can seem rather foolish. It seems to some to be just wasting time on him. But one person's waste is another person's investment. What you waste your time, money, effort and love on shows what you value. If you waste time watching a particular football team, then you value that team; if you 'waste' time with Jesus, then you obviously value him.

Jesus decides to cut in and stop Judas whining about what Mary is doing. He tells him to leave her alone; he accepts her worship, and he also interprets it. I do not think Mary has understood the depth of what she is doing; she is just giving herself to Jesus in the only way she knows. Jesus says that it was intended that she should save this perfume for the day of his burial. It is a prophetic action, looking forward to a time only a few days ahead, when Jesus would be buried and when Nicodemus and Joseph were to put those heavy perfumes around Jesus's dead body. He teaches that what Mary is doing is a way of anticipating and honouring the fact that he is going to die. Jesus lives in the light of what is going to come. Mary, at that point, may not be conscious of this great significance of her actions, but Jesus knows that his death is imminent, and he acknowledges that prophecy for what it is.

If you are reading John's Gospel for the first time, you start at chapter 1 ('In the beginning was the Word...') and think, 'Hmmm, this is quite heavy.' Then there are the stories of Nicodemus, the Samaritan woman and the feeding of the five thousand; in time you get to chapter 11 and start to read that, 'This Mary, whose brother Lazarus now lay sick, was the same one who poured perfume on the Lord and wiped his feet with her hair.' Now the interesting thing is that you have not got to that story yet. You read this and think, 'Maybe I've missed a bit. I cannot remember that episode', but obviously it was very important; then you go back and are unable find it.

Some think it means that either it is very well known to John's readers, or that John wants his Gospel to be read and re-read. Then you know all that happens, and you read the story knowing how it is going to end, and you start to see how all these things connect together; you see how one event has an effect on another. So as you are reading about Mary pouring ointment on Jesus' feet, you are thinking of how she fell at his feet when Lazarus had died. You are also thinking about Jesus washing the disciples' feet in the next chapter, and of the burial in Chapter19; it all links together and throws light both on Mary and Jesus. So the way that John writes the Gospel says to us: 'I want you to live in the light of the whole story; you are participants in the wider story waiting for Jesus to come back. But you also know the whole thing, and you know more than Mary did then; you know how it ends up.' We do know how it is going to end. Yet, although we know more than Mary did at that point, we see her abandoning herself even without knowing what was going to happen; she just gave herself in this most amazing, worshipful way.

We need to worship with the same attitude that Mary showed. She expressed outwardly an astonishing degree of love, gratitude, humility and generosity towards Jesus. That is the challenge to us: that we, too, should give ourselves to Jesus in these ways, worshipping him with true adoration.

*Lord Jesus, when Mary worshipped you extravagantly, you accepted her worship; help me to worship you with a heart full of extravagant love; and so fill me with the Holy Spirit that I will freely express real adoration for you. Amen.*

# 13

# Confession:
# At Simon's House

## *Andrew Perry*

At the centre of this meeting is forgiveness desired and received, expressed in a poignant and heartfelt action.[1]

Now one of the Pharisees invited Jesus to have dinner with him, so he went to the Pharisee's house and reclined at the table. When a woman who had lived a sinful life in that town learned that Jesus was eating at the Pharisee's house, she brought an alabaster jar of perfume, and as she stood behind him at his feet weeping, she began to wet his feet with her tears. Then she wiped them with her hair, kissed them and poured perfume on them.

When the Pharisee who had invited him saw this, he said to himself, "If this man were a prophet, he would know who is touching him and what kind of woman she is—that she is a sinner."

Jesus answered him, "Simon, I have something to tell you."

"Tell me, teacher," he said.

"Two men owed money to a certain moneylender. One owed him five hundred denarii, and the other fifty. Neither of them had the money to pay him back, so he cancelled the debts of both. Now which of them will love him more?"

Simon replied, "I suppose the one who had the bigger debt cancelled."

"You have judged correctly," Jesus said.

Then he turned toward the woman and said to Simon, "Do you see this woman? I came into your house. You did not give me any water for my feet, but she wet my feet with her tears and wiped them with her hair. You did not give me a kiss, but this woman, from the time I entered, has not stopped kissing my feet. You did not put oil on my head, but she has poured perfume on my feet. Therefore, I tell you, her many sins have been forgiven—for she loved much. But he who has been forgiven little loves little."

Then Jesus said to her, "Your sins are forgiven."

The other guests began to say among themselves, "Who is this who even forgives sins?"

Jesus said to the woman, "Your faith has saved you; go in peace."

*Luke 7:36–50*

Forgiveness has been described as 'Christianity's best gift to the world'. We need only think of our families, schools, workplaces, staffrooms, offices and church groups to realise how desperately that gift needs to be offered and received. Yet often we feel deeply uncomfortable, and sometimes extremely confused, about the character of forgiveness. We now think about the meeting at the house of Simon the Pharisee, looking at two features of forgiveness which are expressed vividly there, and then move on to explore a question which troubles many people.

Firstly, forgiveness seems to be *scandalous!* In the Bible, 'scandal' means a 'stumbling block'. The context for this meeting was an invitation by Simon to Jesus to come and dine at his house. In accepting the invitation, Jesus had to encounter again, at close quarters, one of the Pharisees, who were constant opponents. They continually tried to place stumbling blocks before him, in the hope of tripping him up. We may wonder why would Simon have asked Jesus to eat with him. Was it to enjoy his company? Was it to ask sincere questions? Was it to learn from him? Or was it to try to entrap him? Quite possibly it was the latter. Of course, Jesus was aware of this, yet he still accepted the invitation. We can imagine for ourselves considering whether to accept an invitation to a dinner party when unsure of the host's motives. Jesus was pleased to accept, even though he knew that an attempt might be made to manipulate him, and that this meeting itself could be misunderstood.

There was actual scandal as a woman 'who had lived a sinful life' entered the house. In describing her in these terms, Luke is not suggesting that hers were minor indiscretions, but that she was a prostitute, and indeed known as such in that very town. The degree of physical closeness to Jesus of such a woman would certainly have been scandalous to his contemporaries. Most of us, faced with such a situation, would have tended to withdraw from it somehow, but Jesus allows her to wet his feet with her tears and then to wipe them with her hair. That is embarrassingly close. He allows her to pour outrageously expensive perfume all over his feet, too. Simon's response is one we can understand: "If this man were a prophet, he would know who is touching him and what kind of woman she is—that she is a sinner" (v. 36).

If we have been taught well in a soundly Bible-believing church, we know that there are certain boundaries for acceptable behaviour; yet Jesus replies, "I tell you, her many sins have been forgiven", and to the woman he says, "Your sins are forgiven." We might have felt scandalised by all this. Perhaps we would have thought, 'She doesn't deserve it.' Frequently, that is the nub of the problem with forgiveness: we are scandalised, for we tend to think forgiveness is all right as long as the wrongdoer has done something to deserve it. Intuitively, albeit unconsciously, we often behave as though we agree with the principle expressed by the influential eighteenth century philosopher Immanuel Kant, that we should forgive only if a person deserves it. But that is to miss the point of divine grace. The natural human attitude of scandalised resentment is *not* the heart of the Father, nor is it the message of the cross. What we see reflected in this account of Jesus' act of forgiveness is something we so often find hard to grasp.

Jesus understands so well what is in the human heart, and he anticipates the response. So it is that we see repeatedly in the Gospels the teaching and practice of unmerited forgiveness. Forgiveness is not about what is deserved; it therefore often seems to people to be inherently unfair. It is all about grace: God's free offer to you, me and everyone. It is also God's challenge to us—to offer that 'scandalous' grace to others.

Forgiveness is so *liberating*. It is truly wonderful to see the deep thankfulness of this forgiven woman, who in many respects expected her life to be considered worthless. Now she knows that she has not been discarded; she has a future. She expresses the freedom and joy which flows from Jesus in that lovely act of humble service: pouring perfume over his feet.

God's desire is that we should live our lives within the liberating power of forgiveness. It is his best will for us. As we receive that forgiveness each day, we can release forgiveness to others. This liberating dynamic of forgiveness is not only part of our inner life— it is to be lived out corporately in our society, too. In 1997, a major national newspaper published a fascinating article entitled,

*Whatever happened to forgiveness?* The writer argued that whenever a dispute or disagreement arises in either familial relationships or in the world of business, the common tendency to opt for early litigation is profoundly dehumanising, establishing an impenetrable web of sophisticated 'tit for tat' which becomes impossible to resolve. What is needed instead, it was stated, is a rediscovery of the liberating power of forgiveness, for this alone can mean that negative past history need no longer inhibit relationships and business deals. Forgiveness can unlock the future. What an insight from a secular voice!

This is what many brave people in Northern Ireland have been grappling with, and they need our support and prayers as they do so. The issues they are confronting are deep and complex, but many people are recognising the truth that forgiveness is integral to the way forward.

The liberating power of forgiveness is so deep that it touches us in a remarkable way. The restoration of right relationships, made possible as forgiveness is released, has its effect upon the world God has created which has been so marred by sin, cruelty, hatred and lack of love for him and for others. There is often a link between forgiveness and healing. In this woman's case, her forgiveness not only brought healing into her life but also a new and wonderful ability to love Jesus Christ. It was the expression of her repentance and love, which Simon found so offensive: the tears, the wiping of Jesus' feet with her hair, the extravagant use of perfume, the holding and kissing of his feet. All of these actions were the outworking of her desire for forgiveness and acceptance by Jesus. It was hard for Simon to distinguish between her former way of 'loving' and this new devotion to Jesus with its many physical gestures. Simon objected; and at the same time thought that Jesus should not receive her attentions. So Jesus had to teach him!

At this point Jesus embarks on a short discussion with Simon on the effect of forgiveness. So Jesus told a parable which he appears to have used many times in his ministry to encourage forgiveness. Simon could understand Jesus' parable in the terms in which it was put, namely that a man who had a large financial debt forgiven might be more grateful than another who had only a small debt remitted; what he had not done was to transfer the same principle to spiritual and moral circumstances. So Jesus drew out the point with the summary statement 'he who has been forgiven little loves little', so implying that she who has been forgiven much loves much. This, in turn, explained and validated the woman's extravagant love: she had been forgiven much! At the same time, the parable has an implied rebuke for Simon. Unaware of his own failings, he 'loved little'. Jesus made his rebuke uncomfortably clear: "You did not give me any water for my feet, but she wet my feet with her tears and wiped them with her hair...." As was so often the case, Jesus was an uncomfortable dinner party guest. The woman went away healed, restored, forgiven and at peace; Simon to lick his wounded pride and come to terms with Jesus' teaching; and the rest of the dinner guests to ponder their own question: who is this, who even forgives sins?

There is, though, a question still to be addressed. What does it mean to you to really apply and live out forgiveness? We sometimes struggle with forgiveness. We sense that it is scandalous; we know it is liberating; but how can we be real about it? The need of the woman Jesus met at Simon's house was for forgiveness: other needs, such as social acceptance and future employment, could wait until later. Forgiveness was given to her by the Son of God. We all need that forgiveness: it is the overriding, primary need for every man and woman. We may have walked with the Lord for many years, yet there are times when we require not prayer ministry (though that can also be immensely helpful) but to go again to the cross, to Jesus, to receive again his forgiveness, or to follow his example, saying, "Father, forgive them...."

To forgive is not to condone. When Jesus forgave the woman, he did not thereby approve her past way of life; nor did he condone the sins of any whom he forgave. To forgive someone for what they did to you is not to say that their action was alright really; still less to pretend that it did not happen; it is my saying that I am exercising the mercy and forgiveness that God wants me to release toward you—and actually doing so. I may not feel like doing so; it may be an act of the will; but if I forgive really, God honours that.

For all sorts of reasons we can find it hard to receive forgiveness; to really know that we are forgiven. The liberation of the woman came about because she *received* God's forgiveness. It is not arrogant to receive divine forgiveness; on the contrary, it is pride which can hinder us from doing so. We do not rejoice in our sins which make forgiveness so necessary; we simply open ourselves to receive what he knows we need.

Forgiveness—and a constant readiness to forgive—is essential in all our relationships. It is good that at marriage services the wedding party are so often reminded of the teaching in I Corinthians 13, that, 'Love keeps no record of wrongs.' How vital that is, throughout married life. Indeed, this is a truth to be applied in every aspect of our lives. Paul constantly underlines its crucial importance for the health of our relationships, and we need to apply it in the home, toward our spouses and children and in our church groups, too: 'Bear with each other and forgive whatever grievances you may have against one another. Forgive as the Lord forgave you' (Colossians 3:13).

Forgiveness is cross-shaped. It is costly, and can sometimes be excruciatingly painful, to offer. The path to a point of readiness to forgive may be long and slow. Many people carry deep scars and need to know love and understanding before they can release forgiveness. The first step on the road to freedom can be to come to a point of being able to say: 'I do not want to live with unforgiveness in my heart.' On one occasion, after I had spoken at a large gathering about 'forgiveness', I was asked to pray for a young woman who was in great distress. She said that some years earlier she had seen her father commit an awful atrocity against her mother. How could she be expected to forgive him? As we prayed, it was clear that she was not yet at a point where she could forgive him for what he had done, and for how that had scarred her life. However, as God's love began to minister to her, she was able to say, "I no longer want to live with unforgiveness in my heart." This can be the first step to true forgiveness. Forgiveness was costly for God—as costly as that painful death on the cross—and to discover that that was for you: this is the real encouragement both to receive that precious gift for yourself and to release it to others.

The Lord wants us to inhale the fresh air of his forgiveness, and to live in it. It is his will for you and me, just as it was his will for the woman at Simon's house. I encourage you today to receive that forgiving love of Jesus, for, 'If we claim to be without sin, we deceive ourselves and the truth is not in us. If we confess our sins, he is faithful and just and will forgive us our sins and purify us from all unrighteousness' (I John 1:8–9).

*Lord Jesus, thank you for showing us the generosity of your love toward the woman at Simon's house; so that we would know the amazing depth of divine love for all who have failed and gone astray.*

# CONFESSION

*I now confess to you all my sins and ask you to forgive me for them, especially.... [Name anything particularly weighing on your conscience, which the Holy Spirit brings to your attention.]*

*Thank you for dying on the cross for those sins of mine, so that they would be completely and permanently put away, covered by your precious blood for ever. I receive your forgiveness and I thank you for it, for you are my Saviour and Redeemer.*

*Lord Jesus, please show me if there is anyone I need to forgive....*

*I forgive now all who have ever wronged me in any way; all who have hurt or harmed me.*

*Holy Spirit, come and fill me afresh, so that my attitude will be like that of Jesus, and so that I may have a forgiving heart toward all whom I meet. Amen.*

---

*Note*

[1] The reader will undoubtedly notice remarkable parallels between certain aspects of this meeting and that described in the previous chapter of this book. The similarities help to illustrate the unity and coherence both of the biblical revelation of the character of God and the response to Jesus which meets with approbation.

# 14

# Damnation:
# Judas

## Patrick Whitworth

---

Who does the word 'traitor' make you think of? Would it be an apparently harmless old lady living in South London, who believed wrongly that whilst this country was burdened with inequalities it was right to spy for Stalinist Russia? Or perhaps the names of Philby, Burgess or Maclean spring to mind? Or, if you are a little older and have Scandinavian connections, then 'Quisling' might be the name you think of. But it would be widely accepted that the most infamous traitor, or betrayer, in history is Judas. It is his actions that we must now explore.

"I am not referring to all of you; I know those I have chosen. But this is to fulfill the Scripture: 'He who shares my bread has lifted up his heel against me.'

"I am telling you now before it happens, so that when it does happen you will believe that I am He. I tell you the truth, whoever accepts anyone I send accepts me; and whoever accepts me accepts the one who sent me."

After he had said this, Jesus was troubled in spirit and testified, "I tell you the truth, one of you is going to betray me."

His disciples stared at one another, at a loss to know which of them he meant. One of them, the disciple whom Jesus loved, was reclining next to him. Simon Peter motioned to this disciple and said, "Ask him which one he means."

Leaning back against Jesus, he asked him, "Lord, who is it?"

Jesus answered, "It is the one to whom I will give this piece of bread when I have dipped it in the dish." Then, dipping the piece of bread, he gave it to Judas Iscariot, son of Simon. As soon as Judas took the bread, Satan entered into him.

"What you are about to do, do quickly," Jesus told him, but no one at the meal understood why Jesus said this to him. Since Judas had charge of the money, some thought Jesus was telling him to buy what was needed for the Feast, or to give something to the poor. As soon as Judas had taken the bread, he went out. And it was night.

*John 13:18–30*

One of my favourite authors of spy literature is John le Carré. I think I have read all his books. There are few more tantalising portrayals of a spy-master than Sir Alec Guinness as Smiley, the head of the British Intelligence Service, in *Tinker, Tailor, Soldier Spy*. Le Carré is especially good at analysing the complex web of motives that activates the agent, who is prepared to sell secrets to his country's enemies. Understanding the motives for treachery often means peeling back layers of the past, until some incident is revealed which contains the seeds of the treachery. If we were to do an analysis of Judas, what would be his chief motive for betraying Jesus to the Jewish authorities, on a clear night in a garden on the edge of Jerusalem?

The motive is not hard to find, although the interplay of human weakness, predicted failure and satanic infiltration is a more complex web to unravel. We can only speculate about the origins of Judas's tendency to be dishonest. Jesus needed someone to look after the common purse. Exactly how and why a thief was chosen for that position, we do not know. My early spiritual teachers would often use this saying, to impress upon us the rigour needed to prevent our new found faith being corrupted: "Sow a thought, reap an action; sow an action, reap a habit; sow a habit, reap a lifestyle; sow a lifestyle, reap a destiny." This surely was, in reality, the spiritual pathology which fatally diseased any incipient desire in Judas to follow Jesus. His love for money was allowed to develop, like a cancer undetected by any scan. The fact that his previous history was undiscovered simply emboldened him to continue his ways, with an arrogant disdain for Jesus' ability to detect what was going on. In fact, he became more brazen as time passed. So John tells us in a previous chapter of a most revealing encounter, which we have already considered as a separate meeting with Jesus. Mary, the sister of Lazarus, in an action of worship, extravagant generosity and prophetic insight, poured a pint of pure nard onto the feet of Jesus. But Judas objected, "Why wasn't this perfume sold and the money given to the poor? It was worth a year's wages." John adds, with the full benefit of hindsight, 'He did not say this because he cared about the poor but because he was a thief; as keeper of the money bag, he used to help himself to what was put into it.' As James says in his letter, 'Each one is tempted when, by his own evil desire, he is dragged away and enticed. Then, after desire has conceived, it gives birth to sin; and sin, when it is full-grown, gives birth to death.' Judas' disdain for Jesus, and his own self-deception, had become 'full grown' so, one day, impelled by his own greed, he goes to the chief priests with this portentous question: "What are you willing to give me if I hand him over to you?" Never was there a more shabby or tawdry question! What price the Son of Man? Thirty pieces of silver were counted out for the betrayer! So it is that '...sin, when it is full-grown, gives birth to death.' Death was now all around.

When the disciples and Jesus settled down to the Passover meal, there was already a sense of foreboding. This was only heightened by the incidents that took place during this meal, one of which was Jesus' identification of his betrayer. But, even at this moment, it seems that Judas was given one last opportunity to change his mind, or repent. It is this opportunity for repentance, and its link with Judas' later awful remorse, that we must now explore. Then, finally, we must look at the relationship between Judas' own decision to betray Jesus and the prophecy in Scripture that he would do so.

There can be little doubt that Judas had many opportunities to repent of his conspiracy to betray Jesus, but he did not take them. In the Bible, repentance—a change of heart leading to a change of action—is a God-given opportunity. This is clear from a number of instances: Nathan confronting King David with his sin of sleeping with Bathsheba and arranging for the murder of Uriah her husband; Isaiah calling to the people of Judah that, "Though your sins are like scarlet, they shall be as white as snow" (Isaiah1:18); John the Baptist calling in the wilderness for the people to prepare the way of the Lord, and to avail themselves of a baptism of repentance for the forgiveness of sins; and, finally, Jesus arriving in Galilee and proclaiming, "Repent, for the kingdom of heaven is near" (Matthew 4:17). All these occasions provided opportunities to everyone who heard, to have a change of heart and turn away from selfish ways to a radical dependence on God. Wherever the same good news has been made known, from Pentecost onwards, there is a true opportunity for repentance. Judas had innumerable opportunities to change his heart, his ways and his plans, in the days and months during which he followed Jesus around Israel, but he never took them.

After the foot washing ( in John's account) Jesus draws attention to the fact that he will be betrayed by one of them; few words spoken at this meal could have put a bigger dampener on the proceedings than Jesus' solemn charge, "I tell you the truth, one of you is going to betray me." Simon Peter wanted to know who the potential traitor was, so signalled to John, who was next to Jesus, to find out. In the indirect form of identification which followed, Jesus gave Judas his final opportunity to change his plans. This occurred when Jesus said that the betrayer was the one to whom he would give the piece of bread which he would dip in the dish. Dipping the piece of bread, Jesus gave it to Judas and, as soon as he took the bread, Satan entered Judas. This action of Jesus was significant. In giving Judas this sop, a piece of bread or meat dipped in sauce, Jesus was showing him favour. It was an honour to be given the sop by the host, a mark of esteem, or even affection. In so doing, Jesus was illustrating his own teaching in the Sermon on the Mount—to love your enemy and do good to those who persecute you—but he was also giving Judas a final moment to change, to come clean, to confess or to repent; but almost as soon as he took it, Judas hardened his heart in his plan and determined to go ahead. John, with great finality and more than a hint of damnation, wrote that no sooner had Judas taken the bread than 'Satan entered into him.' This is the only place in this Gospel that Satan is mentioned.

With dramatic intensity, no doubt recalling the moment, John writes, 'As soon as Judas had taken the bread, he went out. And it was night' (v. 30). Instead of the presence of Christ, Judas had chosen exile; when repentance would have meant the end of exile, he had chosen instead to go into outer darkness. Judas' exit into exile meant night had come, and the words of Jesus from earlier in the Gospel had their temporary fulfilment: "Night is coming, when no one can work" (John 9:4). Indeed, the only one who could 'work' was Jesus himself, who also prophesied, "Now is the time for judgment on this world; now the prince of this world will be driven out. But I, when I am lifted up from the earth, will draw all men to myself" (John 12:31–32). From the Upper Room, where the Last Supper proceeded, Judas would have made his way to the high priest's house, and from there to the Garden of Gethsemane, to betray Jesus.

All the Gospels tell of the arrest of Jesus, but none more poignantly than Luke, who wrote, 'While he was still speaking, a crowd came up, and the man who was called Judas, one of the Twelve, was leading them. He approached Jesus to kiss him, but Jesus asked him, "Judas, are you betraying the Son of Man with a kiss?"' (Luke 22:47–8).

In Matthew it is slightly different: 'While he was still speaking, Judas, one of the Twelve arrived. With him was a large crowd armed with swords and clubs, sent from the chief priests and the elders of the people. Now the betrayer had arranged a signal with them: "The one I kiss is the man; arrest him." Going at once to Jesus, Judas said, "Greetings, Rabbi!" and kissed him.

Jesus replied, "Friend, do what you came for"' (Matthew 26:47–50).

Nothing could be more contrasting in the respective greetings: Judas, so cynical; Jesus, so tender.

Judas had carried through his plan; the money was his. But having forgone repentance, he was now overwhelmed with remorse, without opportunity for repentance. So Judas goes back to the chief priests, money in hand, in the hope that they would take the money back, so that his now despairing conscience would be assuaged. "I have sinned... for I have betrayed innocent blood," he said. But they refused to take the money; it was 'blood money' and could not go back into the pristine Temple treasury from where it had presumably come! To the minds of the chief priests, the money was more tainted after it had secured Jesus' arrest than before! Judas found no solace from this quarter, and his seething conscience was further stirred by their unyielding retort, "What is that to us? ...That's your responsibility" (Matthew 27:4). He threw the money into the Temple, then went away and hanged himself. The priests were good at squaring circles: not able to put the money into the Temple treasury, they bought a field where foreigners might be buried, and where Judas himself was presumably buried: an exile to God's mercy in a field for foreigners!

What of Judas' eternal destiny? Could he be forgiven? Was he damned? Was his remorse unavailing and fruitless? What did Jesus mean, when he said of Judas, "It would be better for him if he had

111

not been born" (Matthew 26:24)? Is this not an example of Paul's warning that, 'worldly sorrow brings death' (II Corinthians 7:10)? In fact, we are not called to speculate on the eternal fate of Judas, but to heed the warning of his life that we should take whatever opportunities we have to change, to put things right, to return to God, to make amends, to put the right priorities into place in our lives, to deal with the pathology of sin before it sets an irrevocable path to our lives. This, surely, is the only fruitful lesson from the tragedy of Judas' life. The chief priests spoke a true word when they said to Judas, "That's your responsibility."

Finally, we must consider the responsibility of Judas for a crime predicted or prophesied by Scripture. Indeed, Jesus himself uses a scriptural text when introducing the subject of his betrayal, at the Last Supper: "He who shares my bread has lifted up his heel against me." Often, people ask how Judas could have had a free choice for which he was responsible if his actions were already prophesied in Scripture. To answer this question, we must simply explore the relationship between choice and prediction. Let me give an example of how the two could be combined—choice and foreknowledge, that is. Most mornings, I get the children started on breakfast, which, as in most households that are rushing to get to school and work, is not a leisurely affair. Because the shelf is high where the cereals are kept, I ask our youngest what cereal he would like. The choice is between three or four different types, and sometimes amongst them there is 'Coco-Pops', chocolate-coated cereal! It is not hard to predict the choice. But, from his point of view, it is a free choice! This may seem rather trivial compared to the issues at stake in the betrayal of Jesus, but nevertheless the principles are similar. If you add into the equation God's perfect knowledge of his creation, the fact that time and space are of no consequence to him, and that through the Spirit he can communicate with the authors of the Bible (see II Peter 1:21), then it is not so hard to understand how prediction can be combined with free choice; and, in fact, what can be said about Judas in this respect can also be said frequently about Jesus, whose manner of life and death was predicted or prophesied in the Old Testament, but which he freely and voluntarily embraced.

No, Judas was held responsible; and in an age in which we seek to pass the responsibility on to others for our own actions, we do well to remember this. How rarely will people admit their mistakes and apologise—in case, in some instances, it is used as a pretext for litigation. But the result of this failure to take responsibility is a deterioration of relationships of all kinds. I heard a telling and amusing story of a boy being asked by his father why he threw a brick through the sitting room window. He replied, "You know, Dad, it's your genes and the environment." It has been said that, 'to understand all is to forgive all' —but it is not! We may understand a little of how the pathology of sin has worked out in someone's life, but this sort of understanding does nothing to remove from the sinner responsibility for wrong actions; nor does it deal with the root of the sin. The right way forward is for the sinner to come clean, take responsibility before God, and seek his grace, and human help if appropriate, to build a new kind of life. Yes, the chief priests were telling the truth when they said to Judas, "That's your responsibility."

The sin of Judas, in common with the sins of others who were involved in these events, has a *representative* character. The greed of Judas; the envy of the high priests; the eventual cowardice of Pilate; the desertion of most of the Twelve; the denial by Peter; the salaciousness of Herod—all played a part in the journey of Jesus to the cross. The Scriptures teach us that 'all have sinned' (except Jesus) and this truth is powerfully displayed as the sinful failings of the characters around Jesus become apparent at this point. Yet, at the same time, we can see that God works out his plan for salvation—even as sinful men fail, and even as they oppose him.

Whenever we come to take part in the Lord's Supper, the Eucharist or Holy Communion, we do well to recall that this was the meal from which Judas Iscariot went out to execute his act of betrayal. We do well to examine inwardly our hearts, our thoughts, our lives, to ensure that we, for our part, are not betraying, or about to betray, Jesus, whether in word, thought or deed; using those moments to put right our lives with God and with each other, before taking the proffered bread, which is a gracious act of love towards us. We should especially remember, then, that we are responsible for our lives, taking advantage of that opportunity for repentance before sharing in the signs of Jesus' saving death on the cross. Then the warning we are given by the life of Judas will not have gone unheeded.

*Lord Jesus, help me to take responsibility for all of my life. Where I need to be more honest, help me to be so. Where I need cleansing, help me to receive and believe your promise of forgiveness. Where I need to change, help me to do so. And where I need the comfort of another, help me to find your grace and truth. Amen.*

# 15

# Adjudication: Pilate

## Nigel Rawlinson

As Jesus meets Pontius Pilate, we see the culmination of the betrayal process. Pilate's thoughts, and especially his lack of courage, really challenge us today. How courageous are we about professing what we believe? Adjudication is the action of a judge. It is a judicial decision, involving a public declaration. As we look at this meeting, we do more than observe. We participate in the narrative of the first Good Friday, engaging with those events of one day in the life of one man, which paved the way for the salvation of mankind—including ourselves.

A number of events followed the judgements about Jesus which were made by others. As you reflect on these things, think of yourself as one of the onlookers on the edge of the crowd, who watched the drama unfold. You are inevitably involved, because you are there. You will form your own opinion of this man on trial!

We are going to reflect on John, the author of this story; Jesus; Pilate; and, finally, ourselves.

Then the Jews led Jesus from Caiaphas to the palace of the Roman governor. By now it was early morning, and to avoid ceremonial uncleanness the Jews did not enter the palace; they wanted to be able to eat the Passover. So Pilate came out to them and asked, "What charges are you bringing against this man?"

"If he were not a criminal," they replied, "we would not have handed him over to you."

Pilate said, "Take him yourselves and judge him by your own law."

"But we have no right to execute anyone," the Jews objected. This happened so that the words Jesus had spoken indicating the kind of death he was going to die would be fulfilled.

Pilate then went back inside the palace, summoned Jesus and asked him, "Are you the king of the Jews?"

"Is that your own idea," Jesus asked, "or did others talk to you about me?"

"Am I a Jew?" Pilate replied. "It was your people and your chief priests who handed you over to me. What is it you have done?"

Jesus said, "My kingdom is not of this world. If it were, my servants would fight to prevent my arrest by the Jews. But now my kingdom is from another place."

"You are a king, then!" said Pilate.

Jesus answered, "You are right in saying I am a king. In fact, for this reason I was born, and for this I came into the world, to testify to the truth. Everyone on the side of truth listens to me."

"What is truth?" Pilate asked. With this he went out again to the Jews and said, "I find no basis for a charge against him. But it is your custom for me to release to you one prisoner at the time of the Passover. Do you want me to release 'the king of the Jews'?"

They shouted back, "No, not him! Give us Barabbas!" Now Barabbas had taken part in a rebellion.

*John 18:28–40*

## JOHN

Let us look at the nature of the information we have about this meeting. Of course, John wrote this Gospel *knowing the conclusion of the story.* In fact, we must recognise that this is *why* he wrote it. He writes in a style soaked with the intention of showing Jesus as the Son of God, as the means of salvation; as the way of restoration to God for all people. St. John's Gospel calls believers to believe more. He urges us to engage, to go deeper in faith, to grow closer to God. So John writes to convey Jesus to us and, in doing so, emphasises certain things. One is the *truth* of Jesus. He uses the word 'truth' 25 times, 'testify' 33 times and 'witness' 14 times—far more often than any other Gospel writer. The concept of truth in Greek and Roman thought is much like ours. However, the Jewish meaning is far more steeped in religious truth, linking it to the existence, presence and character of God as the Creator of our life.

This is a vivid account. John records many more details of the Roman trial than any other Gospel writer, and in the first person.

This is a record of the *truth*, not only about what was said. Some commentators think John may have been there.

## JESUS

Now reflect on Jesus. He has made the journey from Galilee to Jerusalem. He has left the lake, in the fertile Jordan valley, and climbed the dusty desert road to the city. All the time, he knew what was in store. (See Luke18:31–33.) Earlier, he had set his face towards Jerusalem. He was so filled with compassion and sadness for the city that, as he approached, he wept for the inhabitants. He has had one last meal with his disciples. He has tried to explain why he has to die. His friends did not understand. He has given them last minute instructions, and then prayed for them. He knew that all would become clear later: the meaning of the events about to take place showing the new covenant relationship possible with God —a new relationship that would last for ever. He has just given the sacrament of this new covenant: the special fellowship meal with bread and wine. Judas had left, perhaps only hours before. Once he had gone, Jesus may have felt a new direction emerging. There could be no turning back.

He has walked down the path to Gethsemane. He has prayed, initially seeking a way to avoid the pain waiting for him, if this were in the Father's will, and finishing by totally abandoning himself to his plan. He has returned, further exhausted by this vigil, to find his best friends sleeping. It was too late to explain more. Judas had arrived.

Jesus had been taken back up the steps to Caiaphas' house. A mock trial had occurred—a foretaste of the injustice to come. His friends, for whom he cared so much, have all left him. Indeed, one of his closest friends has deliberately denied knowing him. He had caught his eye as Peter swore away his loyalty with an oath; what a painful desertion that was for Jesus.

So now, totally rejected, utterly alone and exhausted, Jesus has been marched to Pilate, crossing the road down to the valley and passing the Temple on the way to the Antonia Fortress. Maybe, as he went by, he could see the vast walls to his right in the early morning light, and the entrance steps to the hall, where he had been so angry with the tradesmen who had misused his Father's house of prayer. But there was no opportunity to stop. He was being marched onward. The very people he had blessed and healed seemed oblivious to the commotion.

So we see Jesus: alone, exhausted, totally centred on the Father's will. *Jesus, too, knows the outcome. It is his task—the end point and the culmination of his ministry.*

## PILATE

Now think of Pontius Pilate. Focus on the meeting between him and Jesus, which is about to take place. Pilate is the Roman Governor, and resides with his garrison of soldiers in the Antonia Fortress, just north west of the Temple. The Romans were unpopular. Not only were they the occupying force, but they were of a very different religion and culture.

We see that Pilate is treated here as an outsider. The Jews did not come in, because they wanted to avoid becoming unclean. So Pilate goes out to them. Is this power politics? He had no need to go. He could have demanded that the Jews come to him. Instead, he accedes to their wishes. In so doing, he moves to a position of weakness, and so becomes vulnerable to manipulation. He asks them what charges they wish to bring.

This brief discussion reveals the Jewish intention. They do not want a fair trial. They want execution, and this had to be done the Roman way. Jews were not allowed by Roman law to put a man to death. The stoning of Stephen is an exception, but this was done with the approval of a Roman citizen, Paul. We know, too, that the death of Jesus had to be by crucifixion and not by stoning, so fulfilling the scriptures which foretold the nature and meaning of his death. To be hung up on a tree symbolised the curse of divine judgement and rejection. (See Deuteronomy 21:22–23.) John shows that Jesus accepts the full punishment for our sins, the sins of the whole world, by bearing the curse. Remember, as we noted earlier, that *John writes this, knowing the end of the story.* John emphasises this point by repetition elsewhere in his Gospel. (We read in Chapter 12, 'Jesus said, "But I, when I am lifted up from the earth, will draw all men to myself." He said this to show the kind of death he was going to die'.) Such repetition was unusual for John, so he clearly felt that it was a very important point.

Pilate starts talking to Jesus. As we follow their conversation, we see that his first question shows that he has had more conversation with the Jews than John records. How did he ask the question? Did it sound like, 'Are you [really] the king of the Jews?' or 'Are you the [real] king of the Jews?' Pilate, looking at Jesus standing before him, must have found the charge hard to believe.

But was there also a hint of genuine enquiry? Pilate may already have realised that Jesus' opponents were trying to manipulate him. Anyway, he asks a closed question. Jesus does not give a yes/no answer. He opens up the dialogue with a question of his own, so leading Pilate to think for himself. Perhaps he has seen that Pilate is seeking to understand and recognise him. If the question about Jesus' identity is Pilate's own, then we can deduce that he is worried that the prisoner is a rebel leader.

Pilate replies (perhaps riled at the implied accusation that he is a 'puppet', swayed by the masses) that he is not a Jew. However, he is now interested. "What is it you have done?" he asks.

Jesus has created the chance to proclaim the *truth*. Do not forget the Jewish understanding of this word as meaning the deep truth about our origins in God. Jesus opens up new horizons to all who seek. He ends with a challenge to Pilate. "Everyone on the side of truth listens to me."

'What is truth?' Is Pilate jesting or sneering? Did he think Jesus' reply naive? More likely, that question was asked in a rueful way, either because there is no time to discuss it further (this could take all day, and I have to decide now!) or because he is now feeling trapped between the Jewish captors, who want Jesus killed, and Jesus, whom he is now, perhaps, recognising as good—or God? Is this not reflected so often in today's world, where truth competes with political correctness, expediency and hypocrisy? Pilate is unsure what to do! He goes out to the crowd and says that he finds no charge to bring. He has begun to really *see* Jesus. Then comes Pilate's moment of weakness. He does not act on his conviction. He tries to duck the issue and please the crowd, and it backfires. Barabbas was a rebel against the Roman Empire—just the thing Pilate had been asking Jesus about!

Remember that *Pilate does not know what is going to happen—how the story of which he is part will conclude.* We read how he behaved; how he was actually part of God's plan.

### YOU AND ME
Now let us reflect on ourselves. What would we have thought then? *At that time, we would not have known the outcome.*

Imagine that we are onlookers at this trial of Jesus by Pilate. We would, perhaps, have looked on in disbelief, thinking, 'But this crowd was cheering him only last week! Look, there is someone he healed—and even he is shouting for Barabbas!' We may have been afraid, too, with our new hopes of a brighter future dashed. All would suddenly seem lost.

Along with the fear there might be perplexity, because the very nature of the hope that is Jesus would have involved our whole being. We are called by Jesus to love the Lord our God, with all our heart, with all our soul, with all our mind and with all our strength. This is a 'giving' love, and to see what was happening would have been disorientating.

As ordinary people in an occupied land, we may have resigned ourselves with the familiar shrug, 'Oh well, there is nothing more I can do', and trudged wearily home. Consider the feelings of lostness of the men on the way to Emmaus. (See Luke 24:13ff.)

Like Pilate, we too may have been confused, and then swayed by the feelings in the crowd, distracted by the mood of the community of which we are part.

This would be a very sad time, when all hope seemed to have gone.

What do we think *now*? *Unlike Pilate and the folk in the crowd we do know the outcome. We do have the whole story. The judgement we make now affects our lives profoundly.*

Jesus says, "Everyone on the side of truth listens to me." Do we do this, completely, in all things—really listen to Jesus? Or do we have anything of Pilate's attitude in us? The reasons why we so often fail to admit Jesus into every aspect of our lives are mirrored in this story. To profess a faith today, with family, friends, school or workplace, needs courage. We have to stand up for Jesus and that can be very hard. Do we allow ourselves to be distracted, swayed by popular opinion? —or do we want to debate and argue with Jesus, rather than obeying his words?

Use this story to pause and reflect for a moment. Yes, if we had lived then we might have been like Pilate, and we might have thought those things. We might have gone along with the crowd, feeling unable to stand up for Jesus. Pilate made his judgement then. Let us make ours now.

Jesus is alive. His resurrection from the dead is the reality. He reinstates Peter. He is still calling people to himself, and calling those who already know him to come deeper; to know him more completely. So believe in him; return to God; know that the reason he died was that you and I might be forgiven. Receive his love; accept what he did *for love of you* in that historical moment. Gaze again on Jesus: exhausted, totally alone, abandoned by all who knew him, setting his eyes to the cross, preceded by the humiliation of a trial at which a weak-willed, impotent man was the judge. Yet Jesus suffered and died because, "God so loved the world that he gave his one and only son, that whoever believes in him shall not perish but have eternal life" (John 3:16). In Isaiah 53, this fulfilment of God's plan for our salvation is prophesied:

> For he was pierced for our transgressions, he was crushed for our iniquities; the punishment that brought us peace was upon him, and by his wounds we are healed.
> We all, like sheep, have gone astray, each of us has turned to his own way; and the Lord has laid on him the iniquity of us all.
> He was oppressed and afflicted, yet he did not open his mouth; he was led like a lamb to the slaughter....
> For he bore the sin of many, and made intercession for the transgressors.
>
> *(vv. 5–7a; 12b)*

God's plan for us, prophesied by Isaiah, was fulfilled in Jesus. So reflect on this for yourself—and then accept him.

*Dear Lord, thank you for your love for me, and for your patience. You know me so well. If my indecision has caused me to lose my way, and for any occasions when I have lacked courage and not proclaimed you as I should, and for those times when I have let other things distract me from really talking with you, I now repent and ask your forgiveness. Please help me to know that you are near, calling me to you. Open my eyes and ears to hear and receive from Jesus. Thank you for your loving acceptance of me, and for your will to change and sanctify me. Mould me, and direct me, by your Holy Spirit. In the name of Jesus my Saviour. Amen.*

# 16

# Division:
# The Penitent Thief

*Patrick Whitworth*

There were a number of exchanges between Jesus and others which took place while he hung on the cross. All of them were brief, given the agony and spiritual anguish of Jesus. There was a short exchange between Jesus and John, in which Jesus made provision for his mother's future care. There was the underlying communication between Jesus and his Father, which is audible at his moment of execution: "Father, forgive them, for they do not know what they are doing." And then, when the blackness of desolation descends on him, "My God, my God, why have you forsaken me?" There were innumerable cries and comments from different bystanders, but the meeting between Jesus and the penitent thief on the cross was one in which a remarkable exchange took place; and a wonderful example of the effect of Jesus' death occurred. Subsequently, this conversation has given hope to many a dying penitent. Because of the context of this meeting, recorded only by Luke, it may be the most extraordinary one we have considered.

> Two other men, both criminals, were also led out with him to be executed. When they came to the place called the Skull, there they crucified him, along with the criminals—one on his right, the other on his left. Jesus said, "Father, forgive them, for they do not know what they are doing." And they divided up his clothes by casting lots.

The people stood watching, and the rulers even sneered at him. They said, "He saved others; let him save himself if he is the Christ of God, the Chosen One."

The soldiers also came up and mocked him. They offered him wine vinegar and said, "If you are the king of the Jews, save yourself."

There was a written notice above him, which read: THIS IS THE KING OF THE JEWS.

One of the criminals who hung there hurled insults at him: "Aren't you the Christ? Save yourself and us!"

But the other criminal rebuked him. "Don't you fear God," he said, "since you are under the same sentence? We are punished justly, for we are getting what our deeds deserve. But this man has done nothing wrong."

Then he said, "Jesus, remember me when you come into your kingdom."

Jesus answered him, "I tell you the truth, today you will be with me in paradise."

*Luke 23:32–43*

The so-called trials, before the chief priests and Pilate, had taken place. The brief audience before Herod, the tetrarch, was over. Jesus has been mocked and flogged and taken out for execution, his cross being carried by Simon from Cyrene. The crowds followed, amongst whom were his devoted female disciples. The soldiers, under their centurion commander, cleared a path for the prisoners. They made their way to the place of execution, a small hill in the shape of a skull: Golgotha. There, all three were crucified; hands and feet were bound to the wood, nails were driven through wrists and ankles, the upright was then dropped with a merciless jolt into the prepared holes. Cries and curses came, except from the lips of Jesus. From him there was silence, punctuated by prayer. The soldiers divided the prisoners' clothes, gambling for the seamless robe of Jesus. The crowd settled to watch the men die; for some of them the whole event may have been a form of macabre entertainment, whilst others would just have been enthralled or simply curious. The taunts of the 'rulers of the people' which displayed such unwitting irony, "He saved others; let him save himself if he is the Christ of God, the Chosen One", were joined by the jeers of the soldiers. Then the criminals on either side began a conversation, which formed a tale of two hearts.

As always, conversation betrays our innermost thoughts and feelings, and never more so than when we are in extremis. The first man to speak joined in with the jeers of the leaders and some of the crowd. The words of one criminal, "Aren't you the Christ? Save yourself and us!" were sceptical and bitter; derogatory toward Jesus' claim to be the Christ. As far as this condemned man was concerned, here was the moment for Jesus to prove who he claimed to be, in a way that was incontrovertible, by descending from the cross. But running through all these taunts, for Jesus to prove his credentials and claim by coming down from the cross, is heavy irony, for he could not both have saved himself and the world; to save the world required sacrificing himself. So this criminal is representative of all those who look at the cross and see only an empty gesture by a pretender, and so feel empowered to pour scorn on this central figure.

In brief but telling words, the other criminal shows what is in his heart, when he says: "Don't you fear God... since you are under the same sentence? We are punished justly, for we are getting what our deeds deserve. But this man has done nothing wrong." His punishment and imminent death had caused this penitent man to reflect on his life. He clearly believed that he was in some way accountable to God, and morally culpable. He even thought that his sentence of capital punishment by crucifixion was just! In fact he had taken that first step to true belief, which was to admit his own moral failure and look for some form of forgiveness and restoration. Not only had he made this assessment of his own life at its painful end, but at the same time he had made some assessment of Jesus, and had come to some very enlightened conclusions. He could see that Jesus was innocent, and that he should have been suffering the same punishment alongside them was unjust.

Moreover, he felt that his fellow criminal's strictures about Jesus were not only undeserved and wrong, but that they put him in some jeopardy spiritually as well. It is another example that crime does not silence conscience, nor does it suffocate a yearning for God. This has been shown to be the case in our country recently. It is a fact that, in the last few years, Alpha courses have found few more fertile places than the overcrowded prisons of our country! An Alpha supper was held in a prison exercise yard with doughnuts for all, followed by an explanation of the Christian faith!

The penitent thief, this patron saint of all changed criminals, having reproved his colleague, turned with hope to Jesus. He had made the essential first step under the influence of his conscience and the presence of Jesus close by, namely that he was not all that he might be, and that he desperately needed hope for the future!

As he turned to Jesus and said, "Jesus, remember me when you come into your kingdom", the penitent criminal made one of the most poignant requests made of Jesus in his earthly ministry. It proceeded from some realisations about Jesus which are nothing short of remarkable.

The charge upon which Pilate had found Jesus 'guilty' was that he claimed to be the King of the Jews. Pilate had the statement 'This is the King of the Jews' affixed to the cross on which Jesus was crucified. The Jewish leaders had objected to this public assertion that Jesus was the King of the Jews, and John tells us that they asked for it to be changed to: 'this man claimed to be the King of the Jews'. But, on this occasion, Pilate was resolute, replying: "What I have written, I have written."

There were, therefore, a number of clues literally next to or near the penitent thief as to the claims and identity of Jesus. Most probably, he would have heard of the charges against Jesus. It is very likely that he would have either seen or heard of Jesus previously, and he may have heard the row between Pilate and the Jewish leaders over the epithet which hung over Jesus' head. But what is impressive is that the criminal did not think that it was either an unreasonable or unlikely title to give Jesus. In some way, he reckoned that Jesus was a King, even if his kingship was entirely different to any type of kingship he had hitherto known. So when he says, "Remember me when you come into your kingdom", at one level he may have had little or no idea of what he was asking; but the request, proceeding as it did from a grain of faith and understanding, was enough to gain a reply from Jesus which was full of hope: "I tell you the truth, today you will be with me in paradise."

Here was an answer that must have surpassed all his expectations. What, in fact, we have in this reply is the outcome of that spiritual work which Jesus achieved on the cross. That work is variously described in the Scriptures as being an offering for sin, a ransom for our souls, a price for our wrongdoing, a cancelling of our debts, a triumph over the evil one. It was given visual effect, even at the point of Jesus' death, by the tearing of the sixty foot curtain in the Temple, that prevented access to the Holy of Holies. By the ripping of this curtain from top to bottom (signifying a divine action), the way was made open for a relationship with God and an eternity in heaven. So Jesus, knowing that he was about to accomplish this 'work' for which he had been destined as the 'Lamb of God that takes away the sin of the world', promised paradise to this remorseful criminal. In so doing, Jesus demonstrated in the most astonishing way that all we need do, to find such blessing for ourselves, is to ask humbly.

It is worth noticing that what Jesus promised here is quite disproportionate to the request. The thief asked to be 'remembered'; but Jesus said, "You will be with me." The thief recognised that Jesus had a kingdom; Jesus promised him that he would be in paradise—that day. As William Temple remarked, 'The only thing we can contribute to our own salvation is the sin from which we need to be redeemed.'

It is, of course, amazing that this conversation took place when Jesus was undergoing the severest physical torture and such an unimaginable spiritual ordeal.

The meeting between Jesus and the penitent thief is not only remarkable in itself; it is a locus classicus; a prototype of all such meetings. It says simply and profoundly two things to humankind in relation to the kingdom of God: that you are never too late this side of death to enter it; and you are never too bad to be made fit for it.

The reason why both these things are true is because of that word which has cropped up so much in this series of meetings with Jesus: grace!

Grace, as we should know by now, means that he treats us as we do not deserve and gives us what we do not merit; and this on account of his love, which has made up for our deficiency. This love, and this grace, was given in an instant to the dying thief, thereby admitting him to all the glory of heaven on the basis of a 'righteousness from God', which 'comes through faith in Jesus Christ to all who believe' (Romans 3:22).

Put in this way, we see the sheer extravagance of God's grace, the surprising character of his provison for access to his presence. Of all the amazing encounters we have looked at, none drives home more than this meeting that our acceptance by God is entirely based on his favour. Moreover, the same reward is given to a man who had the wisdom to say "remember me when you come into your kingdom" in his dying breath, as to a saint who has laboured long and hard in the mission fields of the world. As Jesus spelt out in the parable of the Labourers in the Vineyard, the same reward is given to the person who has worked all day long in the vineyard as the person who has only worked there for a few minutes. This is not to say that individuals will not be given different rewards in heaven; but all who enter do so on the same basis of *grace!*

So the Church must beware of narrowing grace. Jesus flung the door wide open; it is not for us to begin to close it surreptitiously. Down the ages, the Church, finding it hard to live with this surprising gospel of grace, has been adept at shutting the door and setting in place new arrangements for admission, which gave power to its own leaders.

'Today you will be with me in paradise' are words of surprising joy and confidence from a man who was experiencing the agony of crucifixion. They are said, in fact, to all who hear them and will humbly ask: "Remember me when you come into your kingdom." No one is too bad; no one too late!

*Lord Jesus, remember me, now that you have come into your kingdom. Amen*

# 17

# Stupefaction:
# Mary Magdalene

## *Sarah Couchman*

———

Of all the Gospel writers, John in particular provides the reader with descriptions of some of the most personal and intimate encounters with Jesus. Here we look at the beautiful account of Jesus' appearance to Mary Magdalene in the garden, following his resurrection from the dead. All four Gospels place Mary Magdalene at both the cross and at the scene of a resurrection appearance, so this is a most significant meeting with Jesus. Its intimacy makes it a very precious one.

Early on the first day of the week, while it was still dark, Mary Magdalene went to the tomb and saw that the stone had been removed from the entrance. So she came running to Simon Peter and the other disciple, the one Jesus loved, and said, "They have taken the Lord out of the tomb, and we don't know where they have put him!"

So Peter and the other disciple started for the tomb. Both were running, but the other disciple outran Peter and reached the tomb first. He bent over and looked at the strips of linen lying there but did not go in. Then Simon Peter, who was behind him, arrived and went into the tomb. He saw the strips of linen lying there, as well as the burial cloth that had been around Jesus' head. The cloth was folded up by itself, separate from the linen. Finally the other disciple, who had reached the tomb first, also went inside. He saw and believed. (They still did not understand from Scripture that Jesus had to rise from the dead.)

Then the disciples went back to their homes, but Mary stood outside the tomb crying. As she wept, she bent over to look into the tomb and saw two angels in white, seated where Jesus' body had been, one at the head and the other at the foot.

They asked her, "Woman, why are you crying?"

"They have taken my Lord away," she said, "and I don't know where they have put him." At this, she turned around and saw Jesus standing there, but she did not realize that it was Jesus.

"Woman," he said, "why are you crying? Who is it you are looking for?"

Thinking he was the gardener, she said, "Sir, if you have carried him away, tell me where you have put him, and I will get him."

Jesus said to her, "Mary."

She turned toward him and cried out in Aramaic, "Rabboni!" (which means Teacher).

Jesus said, "Do not hold on to me, for I have not yet returned to the Father. Go instead to my brothers and tell them, 'I am returning to my Father and your Father, to my God and your God.'"

Mary Magdalene went to the disciples with the news: "I have seen the Lord!" And she told them that he had said these things to her.

*John 20:1–18*

We need to identify which Mary we are dealing with. Six women by the name of 'Mary' are mentioned in the New Testament:

1. Mary the mother of Jesus, wife of Joseph;
2. Mary of Bethany, sister of Martha and Lazarus (who sat at Jesus' feet and anointed those feet with the expensive oil);
3. Mary, wife of Clopas, mother of James the Less and sister of Jesus' mother;
4. Mary, mother of John Mark, sister of Barnabas;
5. A Christian in Rome, who was kind to Paul;
6. Finally, Mary Magdalene.

There seems to be a tradition, often reflected in poetry and art, that Mary Magdalene was the woman caught in adultery; a scarlet woman, mentioned in Luke 7:36–50 and John 8:1–11; the woman the Pharisees wanted Jesus to condemn. But it is hard to find any biblical evidence for this. However, there is much that can be learned from Mary Magdalene. Mary's meeting with Jesus was not just a one-off event, but a relationship which lasted over a period of time. So let us begin by looking a little at what her life may have been like before meeting Jesus, as well as at her time spent with him and of course, finally, at this encounter, when she meets Jesus after the resurrection.

# STUPEFACTION

Mary Magdalene is known as 'Magdalene' because she originally came from the town of Magdala on the western shores of the Sea of Galilee. Magdala was known as the 'city of colour'. The indigo plant was grown there, and many dyes would have been produced in that community. Lying by the lake, Magdala was also an important centre for fishing, agriculture and trade. It sounds like a colourful, bustling place, but Mary's experience of living in the city probably would not have been so wonderful.

Luke records that she was one 'from whom seven demons had come out' (Luke 8:2). We do not often use such a phrase today, but Mary is one of a number of people described in the Gospels who seem to have been taken over by some evil, destructive power. We are not told precisely what that meant for Mary, but being demonised meant far more than being subject to temptation, which is common to all. Some sufferers from demonic infestation were dumb; others suffered blindness or epilepsy (though that does not, of course, mean that all sufferers from such complaints are, or were, possessed). They appeared to be insane; their own personalities were supplanted by the words and actions of the demons. We remember the man called Legion, whom Jesus met at Gadara (Mark 5:1–20). Kept away from other people, he was chained up, in order to restrain him from mutilating himself. We can assume that Mary's life, up to the moment when Jesus healed and delivered her, would have been an extremely lonely and frightening one. Ostracised by other people, she must have felt very isolated, and out of control of her own body: a miserable existence. A meeting with Jesus brought her complete transformation.

As we saw earlier, in the meeting of Jesus with 'Legion', the wild man who lived amongst the graves was in the end found at the feet of Jesus, sitting there 'dressed and in his right mind'. A similar change would have come about for Mary. Jesus saw through her strange and disturbing behaviour. He saw what the Father wanted to do in her life: he cast out the demons, and she was transformed.

Many people today need to know that transformation is possible when we come to Jesus. You may not be possessed by seven demons, but if you feel isolated, fearful or out of control of certain aspects of your life, God does not want to pass you by, either. You are very precious to him. He understands; he wants to make you whole. No one is hopeless or worthless. That is an absolutely basic truth of the Christian message. No matter how wretched, desperate, sinful or 'beyond the pale' anyone may seem, God wills that they should know his love; that they should know the compassionate heart of Jesus. This truth was revealed again and again in Jesus' meetings with men and women in every kind of situation, as recorded in the Gospels; and countless faithful Christians down the ages have followed the example of Jesus' love for outcasts, sinners, those in the grip of evil of every kind, and people in special need of healing.

The rest of what we read of Mary Magdalene seems to be a living expression of the enormous gratitude which marked her attitude to Jesus. After her encounter with him which is recorded in Luke 8:2, she accompanied Jesus on his travels. We often think of the group around Jesus as consisting only of male disciples, but a number of women were involved as well, helping and supporting from their own means. (See Luke 8:3.) Mary Magdalene was there on Jesus' final journey into Jerusalem, and all four Gospels tell us that she was present to witness her Lord and Saviour, whom she loved so much, being crucified, then taken down and buried in the tomb. She stayed by his side all the way. Such was her love that she now came at the earliest opportunity (after the Sabbath) to express this love for Jesus, serving in the only way she knew—by anointing him in his death. She had loved and served Jesus in life and she continued to serve him after his death, when everything appeared to have gone wrong. Her love was stronger than the fear which kept other disciples away. We remember that, '...perfect love drives out fear' (I John 4:18).

How quickly most of us forget what God has done for us. We find ourselves talking about what our 'Christian duty' is and grudgingly work out our 10% tithes. But God has done so much for us. Maybe yours was not such a dramatic transformation as Mary's, but he has won so much for us that we can enjoy for eternity, and he is transforming us now. It has been said that, 'If you say, "Jesus is Lord", but your life doesn't change, Jesus is NOT your Lord!' It is good for us to contemplate what God has done for us, and is doing in us, because then we will spontaneously want to pour out our love and gratitude to him, just like Mary.

We can pour out our praise, both in our worship at church on Sundays and as we spend time with God during the week. Of course, we cannot serve and provide for Jesus in the way that Mary did while she was with him two thousand years ago, but there is a way in which we can physically and practically demonstrate our love and gratitude for all he has done for us. Remember the parable of the sheep and goats (Matthew 25:31–46). Jesus praises the surprised sheep for feeding, clothing and sheltering him. The sheep cannot remember serving him in that way, but Jesus replies, "...whatever you did for the least of these brothers of mine, you did for me"(v. 40). That is not just a 'nice' suggestion to agree with, but something to get on and **do**. Choose the unlovely and the unloved. Make time to talk to that person whom no one else bothers with. Sit with the unpopular person in the cafeteria. Find ways your church can try to serve the local community. For some of us it is easier to love those 'out there' than those we have to live alongside day after day—our spouses and children. If that is true for you, then expressing the love, compassion and forgiveness of Jesus in your own home and family has to be your starting point.

So the first thing we see from what we are told about Mary Magdalene is that transformation is possible—and unavoidable, if we really choose Jesus to be our Lord. Secondly, we begin to realise that all he has done for us should result in an outpouring from our hearts of the gratitude we feel for him—both in praise, and loving service of others.

This is love: not that we loved God, but that he loved us and sent his Son as an atoning sacrifice for our sins. Dear friends, since God so loved us, we also ought to love one another. No one has ever seen God; but if we love one another, God lives in us and his love is made complete in us.

*1 John 4:10–12*

Finally, we come to this encounter with Jesus in the garden. The word which sums it up is 'stupefaction'. This is not a word most of us would throw into our everyday conversations, but it expresses well a great degree of astonishment: being stunned with surprise. Mary had come early in the morning, with the other women, to anoint the body of Jesus with the spices they had prepared. The first disturbing discovery for them was that the stone covering the tomb had been rolled away; then an angel appeared to them, saying that Jesus had risen from the dead and that they should hurry back and tell the disciples (Matthew 28:1–7). Mary and the other women did this, then Peter and John came running back, to find the burial cloths lying in the empty tomb. But they soon departed (John 20:2–10), leaving Mary, weeping, back by the tomb—still not understanding that Jesus really was alive, and devastated that someone had taken his body away. Indeed, she is so devastated that she does not even seem to be thrown by the two angels sitting in the tomb, talking to her and asking her why she was so upset! (See John 20:13.)

Suddenly, she is aware of a presence behind her; she turns, and for some reason does not recognise Jesus, but takes him to be the gardener—presumably because of the early hour, and she would not expect anyone else to be in the garden at that time. There seem to be all sorts of clever theories about why Mary did not recognise Jesus. Was it the tears in her eyes, the early morning mist in the garden, or because Jesus was transformed in appearance? Turning from peering into a dark tomb toward the first morning light must have been quite dazzling. But the important thing is not why she did *not* recognise him initially. Far more important is how she *did* come to recognise him: his familiar voice calling her name (John 20:16; cp. John 10:4,14). Like so many deep experiences in life, many words are not needed here. To add to the intimate nature of this moment, John tells us that they addressed each other in Aramaic, which they would have spoken. (Elsewhere, 'Mary' is written in the Greek form). We recall, too, that biblical names often have significant meanings. One might guess that 'Mary' has a very beautiful meaning, but it actually means *'bitter'*. (In the book of Ruth, when Naomi returns from Moab she says to the women who greet her, "Don't call me Naomi [*which means 'pleasant'*]... Call me Mara [*which means 'bitter'*], because the Almighty has made my life very bitter" (Ruth 1:20). Perhaps here, more than just using Mary's name, Jesus is recognising the bitter grief she is feeling.

After Jesus has greeted Mary, and she responds with great joy, he tells her not to hold on to him. This probably does not mean, 'Don't touch me', but rather, 'Don't cling to me'. Mary has a job to do: she has to share the resurrection news with the disciples; and Jesus needs to return to the Father, in order to complete his work.

Jesus' words, "I am returning to my Father and your Father, to my God and your God", are again reminiscent of Ruth's pledge to Naomi, "Your people will be my people and your God my God" (Ruth 1:16). Jesus seems to be affirming that the bond between them is as close as ever, but the relationship, and the work, have changed.

What an intimate, special meeting this was and yet also one of the most significant of all that are recorded in a Gospel, because

# STUPEFACTION

Mary Magdalene is a key witness to the death, burial and resurrection of Jesus. Her testimony provides evidence that it was really Jesus who died; that it was his body which was placed in the tomb, and that it was the same Jesus who was raised from the dead. The vital importance of the historical truth of the resurrection is, of course, stressed by Paul (see I Corinthians 15), so the account of such an eyewitness as Mary is of tremendous significance. What an amazing meeting with Jesus this was for Mary, because in the place of death she found life. Why did Mary experience what I have termed 'stupefaction'? —Because she was *there*! She had stayed; she did not run away and hide when everything appeared to have gone wrong—she continued to do what she could. Do we give up after the first disappointment? If we want to be astonished by the wonder of God, we need to follow Mary's example. We need to hang in there! God is the source of hope. He is so faithful to us. Let us be faithful to him: keep trusting; keep loving. He may give us the miracle we so long for; he may want to do something completely different, but we can be sure that his presence will bring life and light to any situation, and give us the strength to endure.

*Take some time to—*

*Ask God to help you to be more aware of how much he loves you; and ask him to transform you, so that you may know complete wholeness and peace.*

*Contemplate what Jesus has done for you, and how you may pour out your gratitude to him, as Mary Magdalene did.*

*Bring to Jesus any difficult or deteriorating situations which may be on your heart. Reaffirm your faith in him, and ask him for wisdom on how to pray or act.*

# 18

# Hesitation:
# Thomas

## *Patrick Whitworth*

The encounter between Jesus and Thomas was very different from Mary Magdalene's meeting with the risen Jesus, that had taken place in the garden outside the tomb. Like all the disciples, Mary did not expect the resurrection. She had come to the tomb with the other women to embalm properly the body of Jesus, which had been hastily buried on the eve of the Sabbath. She had the surprise of her life when she discovered that the man she thought was the gardener was Jesus; her moment of revelation was hearing his unmistakeable voice pronouncing her name. Nor did the rest of the disciples believe the story of the women when they broke the startling news to them in Jerusalem shortly afterwards. Luke vividly relates that the reaction of the eleven apostles to their news was '...they did not believe the women, because their words seemed to them like nonsense' (Luke 24:11). The unspoken subtext may have been that the women were overwrought, stressed out, the victims of some hysterical hallucinations or, at best, subject to wishful thinking! So the apostles met the women's 'news' with extreme scepticism. In fact the reaction of Thomas differed little from that of the other disciples, but what was different was the emphatic nature of his unwillingness to believe and the clear pronouncement of the conditions to be met for him to believe. All the disciples initially doubted the resurrection until they were given unmistakeable proof, and even then some still doubted or drew back from the truth; the difference between them was only the

137

speed with which they came to the astonishing conclusion that Jesus had risen from the dead. For Thomas there was an emphatic hesitation, from which all of us have benefitted.

Now Thomas (called Didymus), one of the Twelve, was not with the disciples when Jesus came. So the other disciples told him, "We have seen the Lord!"

But he said to them, "Unless I see the nail marks in his hands and put my finger where the nails were, and put my hand into his side, I will not believe it."

A week later his disciples were in the house again, and Thomas was with them. Though the doors were locked, Jesus came and stood among them and said, "Peace be with you!" Then he said to Thomas, "Put your finger here; see my hands. Reach out your hand and put it into my side. Stop doubting and believe."

Thomas said to him, "My Lord and my God!"

Then Jesus told him, "Because you have seen me, you have believed; blessed are those who have not seen and yet have believed."

Jesus did many other miraculous signs in the presence of his disciples, which are not recorded in this book. But these are written that you may believe that Jesus is the Christ, the Son of God, and that by believing you may have life in his name.

*John 20:24–31*

Apart from this incident, from which Thomas got his epithet 'Doubting Thomas', he only appears in the Gospels on two other occasions. The first is when Jesus tells his disciples that he is about to return to Judea or, to be more precise, the area immediately surrounding Jerusalem, in order to see Lazarus, who was seriously ill.

The disciples objected to the idea of Jesus returning to those parts because, only recently, the Jews there, whipped up by their leaders, had tried to stone him. It seemed like an unnecessary danger. But the mood of the disciples changed when they learnt that Lazarus had died and Jesus wished to go and, as they thought, comfort his sisters, Martha and Mary. Thomas' response to both the news of Lazarus' death and the danger of re-entering the area was, "Let us also go, that we may die with him"[Jesus]. It is hard to be sure what inspired this remark. Perhaps it was a piece of bravado, or maybe sarcasm or a genuine act of self-sacrifice to the cause of following Jesus. The remark made enough of an impression on John for him to have recorded it.

The other incident, and remark, of Thomas to be recorded also appears in John's Gospel. Jesus is speaking movingly of his future; indicating that he will be leaving the disciples, but that he has prepared a home for them in the place to which he is going. Jesus then asks what sounds like a rhetorical question; "You know the way to the place where I am going" (John 14:4). In the text it reads like a statement. To Thomas it sounds like a question. The rest of the disciples are silent but Thomas speaks up: "Lord, we don't know where you are going, so how can we know the way?" To this, Jesus gives us one of the most famous statements in the whole of the Gospels: "I am the way and the truth and the life. No one comes to the Father except through me" (14:6). It is fair to say that without Thomas' honest interjection we would not have this crystal clear statement about 'the way' to heaven and the uniqueness of Jesus.

From these incidents we can build up a picture of Thomas—his personality, and the way his mind worked. There can be little doubt that he was not 'one of the crowd'. He would be what we call an independent thinker. Just because all the disciples said that they had seen Jesus alive did not mean that *he* would be convinced by their testimony. He was prepared to ask the question that everyone else thought but was not prepared to articulate. He did not mind that he appeared the odd one out. Moreover, if we put the best construction on his remark of being prepared to die with Jesus in a mercy mission in Judea, he showed courage. Like the other disciples, he had little understanding of the campaign Jesus would be leading, but he was prepared to follow. Thomas was the sort of character who might be awkward to have around; but without him the team would be less strong and less truthful. It seems, therefore, a matter of divine providence that Thomas was not in the room when Jesus appeared to the ten apostles; given his character, he was almost bound to say something outspoken and independent! Of course it was a gauntlet thrown down—both to the disciples to prove their assertion, and to Jesus, to convince Thomas that he had truly risen.

Thomas was moved to doubt for a number of reasons: his own independent, even stubborn, streak; his need for evidence to help him believe (in this he was like the rest of the disciples) and, possibly, a hint of contrariness that prevented him from falling in with the crowd!

Any study of Thomas inevitably leads us to consider issues of doubt and faith. As we have already seen, at the heart of each of these encounters with Jesus there is a central issue; with Thomas it is the resolution of doubt. Thomas was a twin (the meaning of Didymus), though there is no mention of who his twin was nor whether he or she was also a disciple of Jesus. But it has been customary in some Christian teaching to spiritualise the meaning of twins, talking of faith and doubt as 'twins' in Christian living. I would put it slightly differently, and say that doubt is the shadow side of faith. Just as psychiatrists talk of the shadow side of personality so spiritual doctors could talk of doubt being the shadow side of faith. To use an illustration, shadows are at their longest when the sun is closest to the horizon, but when the sun is overhead the shadow is least. In many ways this is true with faith and doubt: when the object of our faith as Christians, Jesus Christ, is most obvious—or 'overhead'—the shadow side of doubt is at its least, but when the Son is found, for whatever reason, at the margins of our life, then the length of shadow is longest.

The truth is that an inescapable feature of God's self-revelation, is that faith is *essential* to relationship with him. "Stop doubting and believe" is not an optional recommendation; it is a divine command, and disobedience to a divine command is sin. If we have been wavering and doubting, then we need God's grace and help to change or to *repent*. The Bible describes doubt; but nowhere is doubt commended. On the contrary, the Scriptures convey a firm and unambiguous message. We are told that, 'without faith it is impossible to please God' (Hebrews 11:6), and that, '...he who doubts is like a wave of the sea, blown and tossed by the wind... he is a double-minded man, unstable in all he does.' (See James 1:6,7). Saving faith which, by God's grace, brings us into a new relationship with him through Jesus, is a gift from him. As we then grow and mature in the Christian life, faith in his promises; faith in his word; faith in the truth of what Jesus has said, is faith that we must *exercise*. The corrosive attitudes of the world around us; the flesh (meaning anything in our thinking, attitudes and will that continues to oppose the work of the Holy Spirit); and the assaults of the devil, can draw us into doubt concerning God's commands and promises. From that place of doubt, the way back to faith, effective discipleship and a restored relationship with Jesus is honesty and, if needed, repentance, which is a change of heart leading to new trust.

In his book *Doubt*, Os Guinness describes doubt as being 'faith in two minds', and recalls a moment of watching a peasant driving a donkey carrying a heavy load. Huge bales of firewood were strapped to the donkey's back as it arduously ascended a precipitous village street. Gradually it slowed to a halt, exhausted. The creature struggled on under a torrent of oaths and abuse until, defeated, it sank to its knees. Guinness suggests that some Christians treat faith like this—when, for example, people are urged very strongly indeed to believe a healing has taken place when really it has not. Admonitions to believe more strongly can begin to seem burdensome in such situations. The best way for our faith and trust in God to flourish is in the context of an open, honest and encouraging fellowship that seeks to put into practice the Bible's teaching. Guinness has suggested that doubt can sometimes be faith which is suffering 'mistreatment or malnutrition'. This suggestion may well be applicable in the case of Christians whose hurts and suffering have led them to doubt God's goodness. We need to know that he can meet us wherever we are, and this can sometimes be at a point of failure, discouragement or doubt concerning his loving purposes. God certainly does not expect us to make a *pretence* of joy when the truth is that we are discouraged. We are not expected to affect happiness when in truth we are sad; nor certainty, if we are racked with doubt and disappointment. We need to end the conspiracy of hypocrisy, so prevalent in many churches, which leads people to pretend about these matters. In our churches we need to help one another, with loving Christian understanding and compassion, to regain such confidence in God's promises that we *genuinely* rejoice and give thanks in all circumstances. Sometimes this will be an act of the will; we may not feel much like it at the emotional level. What matters is that our response to God's love is re-kindled in us by the Holy Spirit, as we become open to him.

So how did Jesus treat Thomas' defiant doubt or scepticism? We already know the answer. He appeared to him and answered him, point by point. They were once again all together in a room somewhere in Jerusalem, and this time Thomas was with them. It was exactly a week later, and still the doors were locked. However convinced ten of them were that Jesus had risen, their basic attitudes still needed to change; they were still afraid, uncertain of the future. Jesus now appeared with, it seems, the express purpose of convincing Thomas. To an astonished Thomas, he stretched out his hand, inviting him to put his finger in the wound made by the nail; and he turned his side toward Thomas, so Thomas could put his hand on the gash, still only ten days old.

Whatever was the mystery of Jesus' resurrection body, the wounds were both visible and convincing. Thomas was commanded to stop doubting and believe. Although overwhelmed, he was given the grace to make the confession of faith, "My Lord and my God!" In a moment, Thomas had been given abundant, convincing evidence and experience.

There are, of course, many reasons why people doubt God's self-revelation in Jesus Christ. At its most hard nosed, doubt can be defiant scepticism, which may occasionally be found in our materialist and scientific culture (not that science itself in any way precludes faith; over the Cavendish laboratory in Cambridge are inscribed the words: *The works of the Lord are great, sought out by all who have pleasure therein. Psalm 111:2.*) There are well known atheists, who use the media to proclaim this point of view. The Psalmist is unambiguous in his reply to such fundamental scepticism when he says, 'The fool has said in his heart that there is no God.' Far more people would identify with the man in the Gospels who said, "I do believe, help me overcome my unbelief" (Mark 9:24). To this larger group, we find amongst the causes of doubt: particular emotions seem still to be undermining our capacity to believe firmly; fear, because trust was abused or broken in the past; misunderstanding of what God is really like; or a form of spiritual amnesia, whereby we forget, or fail to recall, the many blessings of God in our lives; or that, having believed, we never exercise our faith or trust, so that it becomes both weak and undernourished. It is the task of those who teach and minister to identify the cause of doubt, and then to pray and provide the scriptural foundation and opportunities for faith to rise up within us as the Holy Spirit leads and empowers.

Jesus' provision for Thomas of the twin ingredients that dispel doubt and enhance faith—evidence and experience—was, as always, exemplary. Thomas had asked for both, as conditions for his believing. In a special way he was provided with both. He had said, "Unless I can see the nail marks...... and put my hand into his side, I will not believe it." He did see, and he was given the opportunity to touch. That such a doubter was convinced is itself evidence for the truth of the resurrection, along with the many other resurrection appearances recorded in the New Testament. Jesus gave us an idea of the kind of faith God wants from us when he said to Thomas, "Because you have seen me, you have believed; blessed are those who have not seen and yet have believed." The implication is that true *blessing* comes when we move beyond the attitude that Thomas, in his scepticism, displayed. We are to believe in the resurrected Jesus even though we have not physically touched the marks of crucifixion. Thomas's unbelief was not a good place to be, and Jesus helped him to come out of it.

Like Thomas, we too are given *evidence*, and the possibility of experience of the presence of Jesus. The evidence we are given is twofold: the record of the events which form the centre of the Christian faith, given to us in a text, a primary document, capable of being examined, analysed and reflected upon; and the evidence of living witnesses who themselves follow Jesus, and claim relationship with him. This group of living witnesses is immensely varied; it is international, drawn from every culture on earth. Many of those who have examined the evidence, from lawyers to journalists, began from a point of scepticism and ended up with the same conclusion as Thomas: "My Lord and my God!"

We are also given *experience*. What Jesus gave Thomas was, in essence, a *meeting*; an encounter, which would dispel his doubts. A personal encounter is what Jesus offers all who would come to him. Although our age has been influenced by a materialist, scientific and rationalist world-view which proceeds from the Enlightenment, that has proved to be a Trojan horse from which has sprung a deeper yearning for an existential encounter or, put more simply, an experience of *the truth set in the context of relationship*. This is precisely what Jesus offers: a meeting with himself as the Son of God; the risen redeemer, whose wounds are signs of his aching love for us. Jesus turned up in the locked upper room to show Thomas himself; in one way or another he has been turning up in the experience of all those who wanted (or, sometimes, did not want) a meeting with him.

Faith in Christ must be both nourished and exercised. The Fathers of the Church made a distinction between the faith which we believe (fides quae) and the faith by which we believe (fides qua). The faith *which we believe* revolves around the events of God's action in history, reaching their climax in the crucifixion and resurrection of his only son, Jesus Christ. We have the evidence of those events and they are at the heart of our faith. The faith *by which we believe* is the result of Jesus' gracious encounter with us. How that encounter can take place is the subject of our final 'Meeting with Jesus' on the Emmaus Road. The upshot of all true encounters with Jesus is the exclamation of Thomas, "My Lord and my God!" That response tells us that Thomas was transformed. It is thought that Thomas took the gospel of the resurrection to the Indian sub-continent. Wherever God called and directed him, his 'meeting' meant that he went out with a true, firm faith in his Lord and God, Jesus Christ.

*Lord God, I acknowledge that without faith in Jesus, who was raised from the dead, it is impossible to please you; I repent of any unbelief in my heart. Help me to exercise faith in accordance with your Word; give me a firm assurance; take from me any double-minded attitude. So fill me with the Holy Spirit that I will speak, think and act with Christian confidence and boldness and so be effective in your kingdom, in Jesus' name. Amen.*

# 19

# Restoration: Simon Peter

## *Patrick Whitworth*

The main issue in this meeting is the facing and healing of failure. We recall that moment when Simon Peter had denied Jesus in the high priest's courtyard, warming his hands at a brazier whilst Jesus was being 'tried'. Most of us have to deal with failure. It might be professional misconduct, a failed relationship, or regrets over a particular action, or something that only we know about. No one is immune, but some have their failures played out on an all too public stage. In recent years we have witnessed the public disgrace of an American president and a British cabinet minister, both of whom sought restoration through the ministry of the Church. In this meeting between Peter and the risen Jesus, we have the prototype of all processes of restoration:

> When they had finished eating, Jesus said to Simon Peter, "Simon son of John, do you truly love me more than these?"
> "Yes, Lord," he said, "you know that I love you." Jesus said, "Feed my lambs."
> Again Jesus said, "Simon son of John, do you truly love me?"
> He answered, "Yes, Lord, you know that I love you."
> Jesus said, "Take care of my sheep."
> The third time he said to him, "Simon son of John, do you love me?"
> Peter was hurt because Jesus asked him the third time, "Do you love me?" He said, "Lord, you know all things; you know that I love you."

Jesus said, "Feed my sheep. I tell you the truth, when you were younger you dressed yourself and went where you wanted; but when you are old you will stretch out your hands, and someone else will dress you and lead you where you do not want to go." Jesus said this to indicate the kind of death by which Peter would glorify God. Then he said to him, "Follow me!"

Peter turned and saw that the disciple whom Jesus loved was following them. (This was the one who had leaned back against Jesus at the supper and had said, "Lord, who is going to betray you?")

When Peter saw him, he asked, "Lord, what about him?"

Jesus answered, "If I want him to remain alive until I return, what is that to you? You must follow me."

*John 21:15–22*

Peter's denial of Jesus is recorded by all the Gospel writers. Before it took place, Jesus had predicted that, notwithstanding the disciple's words, "I will lay down my life for you..." (John 13:37b) Peter would in fact fail the test that was coming to him, denying Jesus three times. Peter denied knowing Jesus or having been one of his followers. Jesus had said, "Before the cock crows today, you will disown me three times." Luke records most poignantly that moment when, 'The Lord turned and looked straight at Peter. Then Peter remembered the word the Lord had spoken to him: "Before the cock crows today, you will disown me three times." And he went outside and wept bitterly' (Luke 22:61–2). The combination of the cock crowing, bringing home to him his utter failure to remain loyal to Jesus, and the look of pained sadness in the direct gaze of Jesus, must have precipitated the worst moment of Peter's life. No wonder he expressed his feelings in tears of bitter shame and regret! Anyone who has failed in some way will identify with these feelings. In all the excitement of the resurrection, the emotions of that moment, the memory of his denial and the evidence of his weakness would never have been far from his mind or the pit of his stomach!

After the resurrection, the disciples had gone back to Galilee, as Jesus had promised to meet them there. The women who had gone to the tomb on Easter day had been told by an angel to take this message to the disciples: 'He has risen from the dead and is going ahead of you into Galilee. There you will see him' (Matthew 28:7). After further sightings of the risen Lord, the disciples had made their way back to Galilee. Not only had they gone back to the place where they had shared most intimately with Jesus in the early days of his ministry, but they had also gone back to fishing while waiting to see him. At Peter's suggestion, and as on a previous occasion, seven of the disciples decided to go night fishing. They caught nothing. Preparing to come in after a fruitless night, they saw a figure on the shore, who began to shout to them the usual question you might ask any fishermen, except Jesus puts it in the negative, appearing to know the answer. "Friends, haven't you any fish?" They replied that they did not. Perhaps it was at this point they had a thought that they had been this way before! The man on the shore continued, "Throw your net on the right side of the boat and you will find some" (John 21:6). They did as the stranger directed, and brought in a catch only equalled possibly on one previous occasion (see Luke 5:1–11). With spiritual insight, John tells Peter, "It is the Lord!" Peter, true to himself, makes himself decent by putting on his outer garment, which he had taken off to work, and jumps into the water, swimming to the shore! The others bring the boat and the extraordinary catch to the bank where Jesus waited. When they arrived, they found that Jesus was already preparing breakfast, with fish being barbecued! Nobody asked when he had caught enough fish for eight of them! Either then or later, the disciples counted their catch: 153, and all of them large; amazingly, none of the nets was broken! They had breakfast together. We cannot tell what the mood was like around the fire; but, almost certainly, Peter, overjoyed to see Jesus alive, would have remembered another fire around which he had warmed his hands, when a servant girl had asked him a third time whether he was a follower of Jesus. Despite all the excitement in Peter's heart, there must have been a lurking sense of shame and dull despair, which had to be dispelled.

At the end of the meal, Jesus confronted Peter with a searching—indeed a searing—question. We do not know for sure whether this conversation took place in a private moment between the two of them, walking along the beach, or seated nearby; nor whether the conversation was held in the full hearing of the other disciples, who needed to see this public restoration of Peter to his position as the leading disciple. Most likely, Jesus, sparing Peter additional pain and humiliation, had taken him for a walk along the shore of Lake Galilee. The other disciples would have known full well the purpose of their conversation. It appears that John, at least, followed or went after them, for John tells us, 'Peter turned and saw that the disciple whom Jesus loved was following them' (John 21:20a). Jesus' opening question to Peter could not have been more direct. However, not only was this dialogue direct, it was also remarkably formal. Jesus must have judged that this mode of conversation was necessary, in order to restore Peter. He now provided both an opportunity for forgiveness and an occasion for re-commissioning Peter for the future. The conversation was both cathartic and hopeful; the latter being dependent on the former. 'Catharsis' is not a word we use often; it means, literally, 'purging'. As Jesus began this cathartic interview with Peter, he could not have addressed him more formally: "Simon son of John...", a form of address which served to indicate the seriousness of the conversation. Jesus was addressing the bedrock of his identity, for 'Simon' was, after all, his birth name. No mention here of his given name 'Peter', the rock; a name he had so notoriously failed to live up to! It was as though Jesus had gone back to the very beginning, to commission Peter all over again. If Jesus addressed Peter's fundamental identity, he also addressed Peter's fundamental loyalty, giving him the chance to declare now what he had failed to acknowledge in front of the high priest's staff. So three times he asked him the same question, 'Do you love me?' There is no more difficult or basic question to answer. It requires a true searching of the heart before an honest reply can be given. For Peter, the reality of his answer was a little easier to come by. After all, he knew Jesus intimately. He had spent three uninterrupted years in his presence. He had seen extraordinary things. He had witnessed the crucifixion and had seen the empty tomb. Even as they spoke, he could see the scars remaining on Jesus' hands and feet, and could look into the same gaze as had fastened on him in the high priest's courtyard.

The 'flesh and blood' nature of their relationship helped him to reply readily and willingly. Even so, to Jesus' question 'Do you love me?' (using the word 'agape' for love) Peter responded cautiously and conservatively, using the word 'philo' (meaning friendship-love) in reply. Later, Peter, in his Letter, was to marvel at the way the Spirit could generate within the heart of the believer a joy and love for Christ which was not dependent on such physical proximity as Peter had enjoyed. He expressed this kind of loving thus: 'Though you have not seen him, you love him; and even though you do not see him now, you believe in him and are filled with an inexpressible and glorious joy, for you are receiving the goal of your faith, the salvation of your souls' (1 Peter 1:8,9).

The three almost identical questions which Jesus asked of Peter served to overlay Peter's three denials of his Lord, each successive question amounting to an ever deeper probing of his heart and a spiritual stitching of the wound left by those denials. The questions varied slightly in emphasis. They probed the wound of his failure—but in order to heal and bring a new start. Jesus did not heal lightly, but he did heal permanently. Peter could be sure that Jesus would never bring up his failure again; it would be forgotten, hidden forever. But at the time the questions were painful!

Jesus' first question, 'Simon son of John, do you truly love me more than these?' involved a comparison between Peter's love for Jesus and the other disciples' love for Jesus. It no doubt painfully brought to mind Peter's earlier assertion that, 'Even if all fall away on account of you, I never will' (Matthew 26:33). To Jesus' question, Peter now meekly replied, 'Yes, Lord, you know that I love you', or, alternatively, it could be translated, 'Yes, Lord, you know that I am your friend.' Jesus asked again, and Peter replied in the same way. Peter must have felt that the painful questioning was over. It appears that he was unprepared for the third question—at least in the form it was expressed. For Jesus, having asked Peter whether he loved (agape) him on the first two occasions, now changed his question slightly; he used the same word in Greek (philo) as Peter had been using in his reply. It was almost as if Jesus was saying 'Simon son of John are you really my friend?' Such a question, after Peter had twice asserted that he was, must have been especially painful. In his reply, Peter now has to resort to asserting that Jesus, as he knows everything truly, must know that he is his friend. It was this moment that truly hurt Peter, but also it was this question which cauterised the wound of his failure. To mix medical metaphors, the catharsis was now over.

But there is another side to this interview. Jesus had not only to deal with the past but also to deal with the future. In fact, restoration must not only take away the guilt of failure and restore a relationship where it has been damaged, especially where trust and affection has been hurt; but restoration, where a role has been affected, must include rehabilitation. Since it was Jesus who gave Simon the name 'Peter', and the role of leading apostle that went with it, only he could reinstate him to that position in the eyes of his fellow disciples and apostles. This Jesus did in the course of the meeting. He did it by his replies to Peter's assurances that he loved him. Jesus told Peter respectively to 'feed my lambs', 'take care of my sheep' and, 'feed my sheep'. There is no need to build too much into Jesus' slight variation of words; the general meaning must be that the expression of Peter's love for Jesus will be shown in his care for 'God's flock'—his people, or his Church. Those who make up the Church will be either young in the faith or newborn Christians (lambs) or more mature disciples (sheep), and they will all need spiritual food and guidance. Given this charge, it is not surprising to find that ministry to Christians in both these categories is strongly emphasised in Peter's writings. To those who are young in the faith, he says, 'Like newborn babies, crave pure spiritual milk, so that by it you may grow up in your salvation, now that you have tasted that the Lord is good' (I Peter 2:2,3). To those who are given the responsibility of caring as shepherds for the flock of God he says, 'Be shepherds of God's flock that is under your care, serving as overseers—not because you must, but because you are willing, as God wants you to be; not greedy for money, but eager to serve; not lording it over those entrusted to you, but being examples to the flock' (I Peter 5:2,3). Surely these charges, passed on to the Church for which he himself had been made responsible, arose directly from this conversation with Jesus on the shore of Galilee. With these short commands, Peter was given his task for the future and reinstated to his role. But in this process he was forcefully reminded that he could only discharge these duties as a rock founded upon Christ, drawing his strength from him. But there was a final, compelling lesson still to come.

Jesus chose this solemn meeting to warn Peter of the cost of his future calling. Peter would follow Jesus into suffering. The ministry and responsibility that Peter had been given would lead inexorably to a violent and sacrificial death. Like Paul and many others, Peter would have to give up his life for Christ, and in so doing he would share in the sufferings of Jesus. To us, in a softer spiritual climate, such a warning at such a moment may seem hard, but no doubt this last recorded private meeting with Jesus on earth was the right moment to brace and strengthen Peter for what lay ahead. When the time came for his death, he would know at least that this was the course mapped out for him. Sometimes it is helpful to know what lies ahead; sometimes it is better not to know as it only spoils the present, and sometimes God mercifully draws a veil over the future as he knows we could not handle it. In this case, Jesus decided that he would strengthen Peter by telling him 'the kind of death by which Peter would glorify God'. At that moment, Peter's natural curiosity, possibly combined with a measure of relief that the worst was over and his relationship with Jesus was restored, made him enquire what was in store for John. It seems that, for a moment, the clock had been turned back, and once again they were vying with each other for position, privilege and career prospects. But Jesus was having none of that, and so teaches a valuable lesson. It was an understandable question that Peter asked of Jesus, seeing John, his old friend, fishing companion and fellow disciple, following them as they probably walked along the shore of Galilee. Seeing John, Peter asked, 'Lord, what about him?' Jesus' reply is highly instructive and important for our own discipleship. No doubt Peter wondered whether John would have the same destiny as himself; would John also die a martyr's death? Would this be common currency for all who were his disciples? Understandable as it was, the question is not one that Jesus panders to at all. In reply he says, "If I want him to remain alive until I return, what is that to you? You must follow me" (John 21:22). Jesus is, in effect, telling Peter that he is to mind his own business; or, rather, his own discipleship. From this conversation flows vital instruction for all disciples of Jesus—in your discipleship, do not keep looking at what others are doing, nor even envy their path of discipleship. There is no doubt that people's gifts, personalities, circumstances and, above all, calling, will make sure that each of our paths of discipleship is very different. The advice that we must heed is Jesus' simple instruction to follow him. Each has a different race to run. As the writer to the Hebrews says, '... let us run with perseverance the race marked out for us. Let us fix our eyes on Jesus, the author and perfecter of our faith, who for the joy set before him endured the cross, scorning its shame, and sat down at the right hand of the throne of God' (Hebrews 12:2). John may well have died a martyr's death, having lived to a great age and become the elder statesman of the church at Ephesus. We do know that he suffered exile on the island of Patmos where, being in the Spirit on the Lord's day, he saw visions of heaven and his Lord. For his part, Peter was given the same instruction at this, his restoration, as he had been given when Jesus first called him: "Follow me!"

There may well have been episodes in your life when there was definite failure to meet God's standards. You are not alone, for 'all have sinned'. That is why this is such a wonderfully encouraging meeting for all of us. No matter what you have done, said or thought in the past, the truth is that, like Peter, you too can again enter a relationship of friendship with Jesus. Peter had sinned; he had been extremely disloyal, yet true fellowship and a right relationship with God was given to Peter as God's free gift on the basis of a relationship of love with Jesus. By God's wonderful grace, those three confessions of love for Jesus, backed by a willingness to return to the way of faithful obedience whatever the cost, allowed Peter to be restored.

Through the process of repentance; confession before God of our failure and reception of forgiveness on the basis of Jesus' sacrifice on the cross, sins of the past are truly taken away. God not only takes away the objective guilt attaching to our sins, he also restores our fellowship with himself. Often the process by which that point is reached is painful to a degree, as it must have been for Peter; but this is the only way to be restored to God's path if you have strayed from it.

As a result of his meeting with Jesus, Peter experienced the Lord's love and forgiveness again. Through the catharsis of the conversation, his guilt and sense of failure had been dealt with; and, through his sincere declaration of love for Jesus, his relationship with him had been restored. Once again, he had been set upon the path of discipleship, even though, at its earthly end, there lay an involuntary martyrdom. Peter knew the release of forgiveness and the renewed call of his Lord to follow him; the years ahead would show the fruit of this meeting with Jesus, and the joy that followed restoration. That release; that fruit; that joy can be ours, too.

*Lord Jesus, healer of the soul, wield well your tools of love and grace, that as you meet me at my point of failure, I may know your searching love and restoring grace, until I am set again upon the path of truly following you. Amen.*

# 20

# Revelation:
# On the Road to Emmaus

## Patrick Whitworth

Of all the meetings with Jesus we have looked at, this is probably one of the best loved. It serves as a fitting conclusion to this series and an apt epilogue, both because it summarises some of the essential features of any meeting with Jesus; and because its central theme is *revelation*. At the heart of any 'real' meeting with Jesus is a moment or time of revelation, which is life transforming. We could look over the meetings with men and women which are recounted in this book and see that in each there is a moment when the meeting goes beyond mere conversation, or ordinary encounter, to another plane, where the person who meets Jesus is profoundly changed. Their lives would never be the same again; and what took place in the experience of this varied collection of witnesses in the New Testament is replicated millions of times over in the lives of living witnesses who are Jesus' followers today. Indeed, such a transforming encounter can take place between any of us and him, the author of life, through coming to him, or seeking and conversing with him. The term for this sort of 'conversation' in Christian-speak is *prayer*, and prayer is predicated on the fact that, as the disciples on the Emmaus road discovered, Jesus is alive and can be met.

But now we must return to the dusty road between Jerusalem and Emmaus, upon which two dejected disciples were wearily making their way when they were joined by a third person. So deep had they been in discussion about the events that had taken place in Jerusalem in the last few days that they did not notice how this other traveller had come alongside them.

Now that same day two of them were going to a village called Emmaus, about seven miles from Jerusalem. They were talking with each other about everything that had happened. As they talked and discussed these things with each other, Jesus himself came up and walked along with them; but they were kept from recognizing him.

He asked them, "What are you discussing together as you walk along?"

They stood still, their faces downcast. One of them, named Cleopas, asked him, "Are you only a visitor to Jerusalem, and do not know the things that have happened there in these days?"

"What things?" he asked.

"About Jesus of Nazareth," they replied. "He was a prophet, powerful in word and deed before God and all the people. The chief priests and our rulers handed him over to be sentenced to death, and they crucified him; but we had hoped that he was the one who was going to redeem Israel. And what is more, it is the third day since all this took place. In addition, some of our women amazed us. They went to the tomb early this morning, but didn't find his body. They came and told us that they had seen a vision of angels, who said he was alive. Then some of our companions went to the tomb and found it just as the women had said, but him they did not see."

He said to them, "How foolish you are, and how slow of heart to believe all that the prophets have spoken! Did not the Christ have to suffer these things and then enter his glory?" And beginning with Moses and all the Prophets, he explained to them what was said in all the Scriptures concerning himself.

As they approached the village to which they were going, Jesus acted as if he were going farther. But they urged him strongly, saying, "Stay with us, for it is nearly evening; the day is almost over." So he went in to stay with them.

When he was at the table with them, he took bread, gave thanks, broke it and began to give it to them. Then their eyes were opened and they recognized him, and he disappeared from their sight. They asked each other, "Were not our hearts burning within us while he talked with us on the road and opened the Scriptures to us?"

They got up and returned at once to Jerusalem. There they found the Eleven and those with them, assembled together and saying, "It is true! The Lord has risen and has appeared to Simon."

Then the two told what had happened on the way, and how Jesus was recognized by them when he broke the bread.

*Luke 24:13–35*

The timelessness of this meeting is partly derived from it having taken place during a journey or walk. Walking and talking are not only changeless human occupations, joined later in this story by eating, but also they are symbolic of life itself. Throughout the Bible, our lives are symbolised by the idea of *journey*. Our spiritual lives can be seen as 'journeys': sometimes through a desert, like the Israelites in the 'wilderness years'; sometimes with a sense of restoration, as in the return from exile; sometimes as in the journeying of the pilgrims described in Psalm 84 who, going through the vale of Baca (or suffering) make it a place of springs; or, sometimes, like Cleopas and his companion, who were now coming to terms with disappointment, and puzzling over the reported sightings of Jesus alive by other disciples.

The message of the New Testament is that life's journey can only be fully enjoyed and understood if Jesus, who was raised from the dead, becomes the one with whom, and in whom, we travel. There are three obvious spiritual milestones which Cleopas and his friend passed on their journey: explanation, revelation and combustion!

EXPLANATION

The body language could not have been clearer, even before Cleopas reproached the unrecognised Jesus for not knowing about the events that had stirred Jerusalem over the past few days. We are told that the men were sad. When we read of Jesus asking them what kind of conversation they were having, there is a delicious irony, which brings a spreading smile across the face of the believing reader. But the question Jesus asked them provided the preliminary opening, from which he could explain the true significance of what had happened in Jerusalem. They gave him their side of the story; their hope that Jesus of Nazareth had come to fulfil their messianic expectations, but that it had all gone disastrously wrong; he had been sentenced to death and crucified, whereas they had hoped that he was the one who was going to redeem Israel. For them, 'redemption' meant the liberation of Israel and the overthrow of the Romans, the occupying power—but none of this had occurred! Instead, they had heard unsubstantiated rumours that Jesus had been sighted alive by a number of his disciples—some of the women, who had claimed to have seen the empty tomb, a vision of angels and actually met the risen Jesus! For poor, possibly chauvinistic, reasons they might have been prepared to discount the women's testimony—but for the fact of the empty tomb, which had later been confirmed by some of the other disciples (presumably Peter and John). No wonder they were deep in discussion, trying to reconcile in their minds previous expectations of what the Messiah would do. Uppermost in their thinking was the seemingly tragic death of Jesus, and the rumours of his resurrection, which recalled some of the Lord's sayings, which they dimly remembered, that he would rise on the third day! Into their confusion Jesus added the necessary explanation.

Jesus had to rework their perspective—their messianic understanding—before the two disciples could grasp the truth that the crucifixion of the Messiah, and his subsequent resurrection, had always been God's plan and could be found in the Scriptures, if they are understood rightly.

The two disciples needed spiritual sight to see a new picture of what the Messiah would do. In their case, this new understanding was brought to light by Christ himself. Jesus no doubt pulled together the picture of the Servant suffering for his people (to be found principally in Isaiah 53) and the majestic picture of the Son of Man found in Daniel. As he spoke, their minds were illuminated and their hearts burned! But they needed this explanation; they had to understand that the death and sufferings of Jesus were indeed the means whereby he would redeem Israel. But the Israel he redeemed would no longer be merely a single nation state or an individual race but a New Israel, comprising all who were to place their hope of forgiveness and restoration in the death and resurrection of the Messiah.

Similarly, today, we cannot truly believe without understanding this explanation and realising, as the Good Friday hymn deftly puts it: 'We may not know, we cannot tell, what pains he had to bear, but we *believe* it was for us he hung and suffered there.' To put it simply, he died for our redemption; for our forgiveness, which must be personally claimed. So *explanation* is an important prerequisite to true faith, and that means explanation in each generation and to each person. Jesus did not first overwhelm them with his resurrection presence; he respected their minds, and showed the importance of a right understanding, taking time to explain the events upon which faith is to be based. If you understand, then rejoice; but if you are still seeking understanding, join an Alpha course, or something similar, where explanation can be given. Remember that in the parable of the sower, the seed that produced much fruit was the word which was received, understood, and allowed to grow.

## REVELATION

At the heart of this meeting lies the action of *revelation*. At the beginning of the encounter, when Jesus drew alongside the two engrossed disciples, we are told by Luke that their eyes were restrained, so that they did not know Jesus. This implies that God acted upon them, temporarily preventing recognition. Later, in the account, when Jesus is sitting at the table with them, he took bread, blessed and broke it, and gave it to them. It was *then* that their eyes were opened; suddenly they knew him, and then he vanished from their sight. Although the moment of recognition came when Jesus performed his characteristic actions of taking, thanking, breaking and distributing the bread, the process of revelation was taking place from the moment Jesus joined them on the way. This revelation took place in the context of companionship.

'Companionship', as we know, refers to association with, or accompanying, another; but its root meaning is derived from its two parts, 'com' and 'panis'; and as my old school Smith's Latin dictionary tells me, 'panis' means 'coarse or household bread'; 'com' means together. Such an understanding of companionship helps us to see its deepest meaning: the sharing of food together. Jesus reserved the moment of recognition for when he shared bread with them and ate with them. Throughout the Bible, meals are invested with huge significance, so that they become indisputably the greatest symbol of friendship and companionship. It is not surprising that, as he did here, Jesus chose a meal—the Lord's Supper, Holy Communion or Eucharist—as the occasion not only for remembrance of his redeeming death, but also of sharing *himself* with us.

During this meal with Cleopas and his companion, at the exact moment when Jesus performed the familiar action of taking, thanking and breaking the bread, they recognised him or, to put it the other way, Jesus was revealed to them and their previous 'blindness' was removed.

There are two sides to this moment of recognition: God revealing his Son; and the disciples' desire to understand. Matthew records the earlier words of Jesus, "All things have been committed to me by my Father. No one knows the Son except the Father, and no one knows the Father except the Son and those to whom the Son chooses to reveal him" (Matthew 11:27). In other words, Father and Son reveal each other to humankind; and to whom do they reveal themselves? —to those who want to understand; to those who come to Jesus. In the verse immediately following, Jesus added his words of invitation: "Come to me, all you who are weary and burdened, and I will give you rest" (Matthew 11:28). Cleopas and his friend had demonstrated their desire to understand, as well as their longing for the companionship of this (as yet unknown) fellow traveller by 'constraining' Jesus to stay with them, because it was nearly evening.

The moment of recognition was, therefore, a convergence of their desire to understand and the Father's willingness to reveal his now risen Son to them. This combination of human desire to know the meaning of these events described in the Gospels, and the Father's willingness to reveal his Son to all who come to him, is the common basis for any real encounter with Jesus.

As soon as this moment of recognition had taken place and Jesus had disappeared, the two disciples reflected on the feeling in their hearts those last few hours, which they summed up by saying, "Were not our hearts burning within us while he talked with us on the road and opened the Scriptures to us?" There was a feeling of *spiritual combustion* in their hearts.

COMBUSTION
The French mathematician Blaise Pascal, who produced a treatise on conic sections which laid the groundwork for projective geometry, and who invented, amongst other things, a barometer, a hydraulic press and a calculating machine, came to a moment of despair in his life. Then on 23rd November 1654, he had an extraordinary experience of God, which he described as, 'Fire, fire, fire; joy, joy, joy, tears of joy.' He wrote those words on a piece of paper, then hid it in the lining of his cloak for the rest of his life.

Although a meeting with Jesus is not always so emotional or ardent, the two disciples on the Emmaus road clearly experienced something similar. They had burning hearts as they listened to Jesus explaining from the Scriptures why it was necessary for him to suffer before entering his glory. It is not unknown to have such feelings of spiritual heat! I well remember some years ago experiencing what could only be described as a 'burning heart', as some passages from Paul's second letter to the Corinthians were explained; and many who have been prayed for by others have experienced an almost tangible sensation of heat in their bodies. These are sometimes signs that, through the ministry of the word and the prayers of believers, the Spirit of Christ is assuring, equipping and encouraging his people today, on their journey through life.

The effect of this meeting upon the disciples was immediate. They did not stay the night at the village of Emmaus, but straight away made their way back to Jerusalem to tell their news. In effect, they were made both witnesses to the resurrection, and evangelists as well. Their feet could no longer stay in one place and their tongues could not be tied; they had good news to spread.

Such is the effect of a real and authentic meeting with Jesus: now we have an explanation for the cross and resurrection; we have *recognised* Jesus as the Son of God; and now we have 'news' to tell. When the two disciples arrived back in Jerusalem, they 'told what had happened on the way'. When we have had our own meeting with Jesus, we find that we, too, are 'fired' to tell of how he has accompanied us along the way. It was this *combustion* that turned the world upside down! If you have accepted Jesus Christ as your Lord and Saviour, then you have a story of what has happened to you 'on the way'. Its centrepiece is that meeting with him who is 'the way, the truth and the life'. Like those disciples to whom Jesus revealed himself, *you* are called to be a witness to the same risen Lord. The Holy Spirit will release in you that fire which is needed in every disciple, if you ask him to do so, and then go on being filled with him, day by day.

*Lord Jesus, who graciously revealed yourself as the risen Lord, in the breaking of bread, open my eyes that I may see your presence accompanying me along the way; open my mind, that I may understand your suffering as the way to glory; and put your fire in my heart, that I might be a faithful, effective witness and an obedient disciple, all the days of my life. Amen.*

# *More good books from Terra Nova Publications:*

*Canadian prices are indicated in brackets*

SERVANTS OF THE LIVING GOD   Peter H. Lawrence, John Woolmer and others
Foreword by David Pytches
ISBN 1901949044  £5.99 ($14.95)

THE HOT LINE   Peter H. Lawrence
Foreword by David Pytches   Preface by Michael Green
ISBN 0952268868  £5.99 ($14.95)

THE STRUGGLE: THE BATTLE BETWEEN FLESH AND SPIRIT   Hartmut Kopsch
ISBN 190194901X  £7.99 ($19.95)

HEALING AT THE WELL   Mike Endicott
Foreword by Jennifer Rees Larcombe   Preface by the Archbishop of Wales
ISBN 1901949079  £7.99 ($19.95)

TRUST YATES!   Mike Endicott
Stories of a guide dog with a dog collar
Foreword by Adrian Plass
ISBN 1901949087  £5.99 ($14.95)

LIVING FAITH   Don Latham
ISBN 1901949125  £7.99 ($19.95)

EVERYDAY FAITH   Don Latham
ISBN 1901949109  £3.50 ($8.95)

A FAITH THAT WORKS   Don Latham
ISBN 1901949001  £6.99 ($16.95)

BEING UNMISTAKABLY CHRISTIAN AT WORK   Don Latham
ISBN 1901949060  £3.50 ($8.95)

GROWING IN THE WORD   Hilary Latham
ISBN 1901949028  £5.99 ($14.95)

GOD AND THE TROUBLES OF LIFE   Paul Griffiths
ISBN 1901949095  £6.99 ($16.95)

DOING WHAT COMES SUPERNATURALLY   Peter H. Lawrence
ISBN 0952268841  £5.99 ($14.95)

FROM FREEMASONRY TO FREEDOM   Stanley Trickett
ISBN 1901949052  £4.50 ($11.25)

TOWARDS CHRISTIAN MATURITY   Hilary Latham
ISBN 0953149412  £6.95 ($16.95)

---

Available from Christian bookshops throughout the UK
In Canada, from the Anglican Book Centre, Toronto
In Australia, from Koorong Books